Fire, Water, and Wind

Fire, Water, and Wind

God's Transformational Narrative

Learning from Narrative Psychology, Neuroscience, and Storytelling about Identity Formation

Norbert Haukenfrers

Foreword by Leonard Sweet

WIPF & STOCK · Eugene, Oregon

FIRE, WATER, AND WIND
God's Transformational Narrative: Learning from Narrative Psychology, Neuroscience, and Storytelling about Identity Formation

Copyright © 2016 Norbert Haukenfrers. All rights reserved. Except for brief quotations in critical publications or reviews, no part of this book may be reproduced in any manner without prior written permission from the publisher. Write: Permissions, Wipf and Stock Publishers, 199 W. 8th Ave., Suite 3, Eugene, OR 97401.

Wipf & Stock
An Imprint of Wipf and Stock Publishers
199 W. 8th Ave., Suite 3
Eugene, OR 97401

www.wipfandstock.com

PAPERBACK ISBN 13: 978-1-4982-1988-4
HARDCOVER ISBN 13: 978-1-4982-1990-7

Manufactured in the U.S.A.   05/06/2016

Scripture taken from *The Message*. Copyright © 1993, 1994, 1995, 1996, 2000, 2001, 2002. Used by permission of NavPress Publishing Group.

THE HOLY BIBLE, NEW INTERNATIONAL VERSION®, NIV® Copyright © 1973, 1978, 1984, 2011 by Biblica, Inc.® Used by permission. All rights reserved worldwide.

To Teresa, my wife and best friend.

You give more than I will ever be able repay.

Thank-you

To Jasohna and Ellora

Know that I will always love you

Thank you for your support and encouragement.

"The Word at all times and all places desires
to become flesh."

MAX THE CONFESSOR

Contents

Foreword by Leonard Sweet | ix
Acknowledgments | xiii
Introduction: Getting Down | xv

Part 1: Narrative Psychology and Neuroscience | 3
1 Narrative Psychology | 5
2 Neuroscience | 26

Part 2: Story Matters | 41
3 Why Story | 43
4 Culture | 48
5 What is a Story? | 52
6 What Kind of Stories? | 55

Part 3: Artisan's of Identity | 61
7 Biblical Story | 63
8 The Story of Self | 66
9 A Biblical Imagination | 73
10 Conclusion | 76

Bibliography | 81

Foreword

WHEN I CAN TELL your story to someone in front of you, and you can tell my story to someone in front of me, it is a holy moment. When I can tell God's story in you to someone in front of you, and you can tell God's story in me to someone in front of me, we have now entered the holy-of-holies.

A survivor of the Johnstown Flood ("The Great Flood of 1899") was fond of telling the story to anyone who would listen. With each telling, of course, the story became more embellished. He finally died of old age and went to heaven. When he had settled in, St. Peter stopped by to ask if everything came up to his expectation. "It's great here," the man said, "But I surely would like to tell the story of the Johnstown Flood to some of the others up here." St. Peter obliged. He assembled a large, heavenly audience. But as the man rose to address them, St. Peter whispered in his ear, "I think I'd better warn you: Noah is in the audience."

A story told often is not always a story told true, or well. It is not just what stories we tell, but how well we tell those stories, that shapes the unfolding of our stories. We need to tell better, deeper, more complex stories about how each of us lives and feels and experiences our lives.

If we want to talk about the deepest things of life, we must break through the language barrier and enter the world of art, music, festival, story, and image. One reason Jesus told truth in story form is that some truths cannot be communicated any other way.

Foreword

The materiality and medium of story are necessary for the message of Truth.

> You want to know about the kingdom of night? There is no way to describe the kingdom of night. But let me tell you a story. You want to know about the condition of the human heart? There is no way to describe the condition of the human heart. But let me tell you a story. . . You want a description of the indescribable? There is no way to describe the indescribable. But let me tell you a story.
>
> —Elie Wiesel, Novelist/Nobel laureate/Holocaust survivor

How we sustain meaning, morality, and what matters in our lives is through narratives built on metaphors. Your mind is like a closet with hangers. Each hanger is a metaphor that carries a story. Empty closets and empty souls have no hangers. Strong identities come from full closets.

J. Edward Chamberlain has studied the historic interaction of Anglos and First Nations people in Canada, and has summarized the difference in the provocative title of his 2004 book. Anglo settlers claimed land based on a piece of paper called a "title" that "entitled" you to some property. First Nations people could not understand how a white leaf with some writing on it could prove ownership of anything, much less land. When told to get off the land because of a "title," one chief demanded of the "law" enforcers an answer to this question, which became the title of Chamberlain's book: "If this is your land, where are your stories?"

Stories function as memes, which means they reproduce, and have organic life. The world offers us narrative memes of narcissism, cynicism, and nihilism (fear); Christ offers us narrative memes of relationship, creativity, and hope (love). We choose which we'll believe, but once we've chosen, the narrative becomes our lens, and will color all our perceptions, and therefore either limit or open our options.

We don't need to explain a story, since a good story rarely wastes time explaining itself, and Jesus told the best stories of anyone in history. We don't have to worry about making the Jesus story come out right. We don't have to make meaning in life, or

Foreword

heroically create meaning out of meaninglessness, since life is full of meaning. Each one of us must find our part and place in the great, good, never-ending story and then trust the story with our lives.

There is a reason a story or parable accompanies almost every law, commandment, or moral principle in the Talmud and Midrash. The Bible is not a rulebook of moral values, worldviews, classical virtues, or isolated verses, but a storybook of relationships, revelations, and mysteries. In fact, every detail and plot device of The Sacred Story unveils a mystery. Yet we cram minds with facts rather than rapture souls with mystery.

Norbert Haukenfrers has written a marvelous book on the need for the church to rediscover its identity in some of its most primal and primary metaphors. The earliest creation account in the Bible starts with three images, and quickly adds a fourth. The first three metaphors in the Bible are earth, water, and wind. Add fire, and these four elements constitute the creative life force of Jewish-Christian cosmology. This was symbolized in the curtain that walled off the holy-of-holies, a five inch tapestry with a tight weave that brought together these four elements of earth, water, wind, and fire. But the greatest contribution of this book is its demonstration that it's not enough to learn to think and talk in story, and to learn to be a storyteller. The church needs to become a culture of storytellers, creating stories worth telling. This used to be called "testimony time." If it takes a thousand voices to tell a single story, it takes all our voices to tell the Jesus story. The better the storytelling, the more Jesus the church.

John Knox (1513–1572), the leader of the Protestant Reformation in Scotland and the founder of Scottish Presbyterianism, has recently been reinvented for the 21st century. Known for his long and tightly argued sermons, his house in Edinburgh has been a beloved mecca for Scottish Presbyterianism in particular, and Reformation Protestantism in general. Recently Knox's home underwent a reframing. It is now known as the Scottish Storytelling Center, "the world's first purpose-built modern center for live storytelling." Norbert Haukenfrers is advocating a similar reinventing and reframing for our 22nd century kids.

St. Augustine's four-volume classic *On Christian Doctrine* (397, 426) is a showcase on how these four images have shaped the doctrines of the faith. At one point in volume four Augustine exegetes the simple image of the cup of cold water given in Jesus' name.

> Is it not the case that when we happen to speak on this subject to the people, and the presence of God is with us . . . a tongue of fire springs out of the cold water which inflames every cold human hearts with a grace for doing good in hope of eternal life? (IV.18.37)

Haukenfrers has written a book so bold and beautiful that flames of fire leap out of the images of cups of cold water, and from the images of earth and wind as well.

—Leonard Sweet, best-selling author, professor (George Fox University, Tabor College, Drew University), and chief architect and contributor to preachthestory.com

Acknowledgments

To God be the glory, for the great things he is doing.

To Teresa, your enduring, wild love is challenging and changing me.

To Jasohna and Ellora, for your support and encouragement. Over the years you have given me time, for this and other work, that could have been spent together; without your incredible love, support and encouragement I would not be the man I am today.

To my parents and grandparents for the gift of faith and love.

To my friends in the Semiotics and Future Studies program at George Fox University; Patrick Sehl, Matthew Thomas, Rob Parker Bryce Ashlin-Mayo, Greg Borror, Shane Sebastian, Danny Russel, Doug Withrup Paula Champion Jones, Kevin Glenn, Scott Ness, Len Calhoun, Rick Callahan, Phil Newell, Loren Kerns, Clifford Berger, and Rob Clark, thank you. As iron sharpens iron you have challenged me in an environment of love, respect, and trust.

To my Teachers, Pastors, and Mentors: Rick Wiebe, Ron Pettigrew, Richie White, Fred Friesen, Norman Reimer, Eugene Peterson, J. I. Packer, James Houston, Lorne Wilkinsons and Leonard Sweet, as well as the teachers through the ages that have understood their times.

Acknowledgments

To the editors and commentators of this work, thank you, you have improved the arguments and aided with clarity. Anything that remains challenging, unclear, or questionable is solely my error, ignorance, or oversight.

Introduction
Getting Down

JENNY GRADUATED FROM HER village's high school at the top of her class and enrolled that fall at the nearest community college with dreams of becoming a lawyer. She dropped out after one semester because she could not do the work; she was not prepared. In the spring, she returned to her village on the Indian Reservation with her hopes and dreams crushed, only to be received by the mocking taunts of her high school friends.

In her mind there was no point in trying, there was no way to escape; change was not possible.

She joined her friends, who had never left the village, drowning her shame with alcohol, and exchanging her dreams for the erotic, because she just wanted the emptiness to stop. It was more than she could accept; by the fall, a year after her return, everything was raw and ragged. Come winter, she could no longer dull her pain by drowning in alcohol. She found relief in the needle of a friend.

The following spring, she discovered that she was expecting a child and infected with HIV. She had a pretty good idea of who the father might be, but couldn't be sure. But was it him or someone else that gave her this dreaded disease, or was it from one of the many-shared needles? What did it matter, anyways? What was the point in continuing? Her indifference was growing. What right does she have to bring a kid into her messy life? Is there a way to end the shame and stop the pain?

Introduction

As a pastor living in Saskatchewan, this story is all too real. Saskatchewan reserves have an HIV infection rate 11 times higher than the national average,[1] and among First Nations people (refers to aboriginal peoples living in Canada who are neither Inuit nor Métis) living on reserve, the HIV infection rate has doubled since 2009.[2] Dr. Mona Loutfy, an infectious disease specialist at Women's College in Toronto has gone so far as to say that, "You don't need to go to Africa to do HIV humanitarian work. You can go to Saskatchewan."[3] Coupled to these infection rates is a deluge of despair and hopelessness that is driving the wreckage of suicide occurring on Canadian First Nations Reserves, with five to seven times as many suicides as the rest of the country.[4]

Part of this may be understood when placed within a historical context of the establishment of Indian Residential Schools shortly after Canada's Indian Act of 1876 and the amendments of 1884 becoming law. These schools, while funded by the federal government, were operated mostly by the Roman Catholic Church of Canada and the Anglican Church of Canada. The primary objective of these schools was removing and isolating Indian children from the influence of their families, traditions, and culture—to assimilate them into the dominant European culture of the day.

---

1. http://www.cbc.ca/m/news/canada/saskatchewan/hiv-epidemic-sweeping-saskatchewan-reserves-1.3097212. Accessed September 8, 2015.

2. The new infection rate in 2012: 17.2 per 100,000; and in 2011, it was 19.1 per 100,000. The Canadian average is 7.4 per 100,000. 2012 HIV/AIDS Statistics released at Prairie HIV Conference, Travel Lodge, Saskatoon SK, November 4–5, 2013.

3. http://www.cbc.ca/m/news/canada/saskatchewan/hiv-epidemic-sweeping-saskatchewan-reserves-1.3097212.

4. In 2009, "According to Health Canada, suicide rates are five to seven times higher in First Nations communities than in the rest of Canada. In extreme cases, some aboriginal communities have seen suicide rates 800 times higher than the national average." http://www2.canada.com/saskatoonstarphoenix/news/third_page/story.html?id=fba8ea08-3183-4ea8-be1a-c3bd54c87cb9 (accessed November 6, 2013). In 2009, the Canadian national average was 11.5 suicides per 100,000. Remembering that suicides are only counted as suicides if it can be the demonstrated cause of death recorded, the overall average is likely higher.

Introduction

As is infamously remembered, the sole objective was, "To kill the Indian in the child."[5] Add to the already atrocious intentions of these schools, the observations found in Dr. Bryce's Report submitted in 1907, as the Medical Inspector for the Department of Indian Affairs, where he observes that of the 150,000 aboriginal children who attended, somewhere between 90 and 100 percent, experienced physical, emotional, and sexual abuse while in the care of these institutions that had a 40 to 60 percent mortality rate. The last of these schools closed in 1996.

To say that Prince Albert is a place where many people are in crisis and have experienced deep hurt is not difficult. What does it mean to be a church here that participates in the mission of God and offers forgiveness, hope, and the power to change?

While there have been official apologies made by government and church leaders, compensation claims paid to survivors, and A Truth and Reconciliation Commission Report, the healing and reconciliation is just beginning. The memory of residential schools, for many, is one of isolation, separation, and abusive treatment. This memory and the sweeping effects of the Indian Acts of the late nineteenth century are often cited as why many learned to self-abuse and fail to love themselves, their families, and their indigenous languages and cultures. Prince Albert, Saskatchewan is not unique in this pain; every community with First Nations peoples in Canada has been affected. This painful denial and loss of identity is continuing to fester with the aid of low education standards, alcohol and narcotic addictions, and high crime and incarceration rates, as well as other dynamics, according to The Truth and Reconciliation Commission of Canada: Interim Report. The pandemic of receiving and inflicting pain with all its symptomatic manifestations, expressing this deep level of despair and hopelessness, cannot be denied. Something must be done. *My proposal is for a reintroduction of a narrative intelligence that can play a key role in the required re-formation of a people's identity.*

---

5. http://indigenousfoundations.arts.ubc.ca/home/government-policy/the-residential-school-system.html.

Introduction

We need to be telling the stories; stories not only of what happened and how survival was achieved, but stories that are offering people release from the shackles of pain and abuse of the past and present (redemption), stories offering people hope and the possibility of living into a new story (transformation). As the Anglican Church of Canada's National Indigenous Bishop, Mark MacDonald shared with me in an interview that, "The truth, the whole truth and nothing but the truth needs to be told and we need to do this by telling stories, as stories simply have more room for truth."[6] It is in stories that we find "a spark, a power: to comfort, connect, destroy, transform—and even heal."[7] It is through stories where people truly connect with one another and create community. Those of us who follow Jesus have a reason to want to connect because we are part of the greatest story of redemption and transformation ever told.

Part of this storytelling process for me has been that my perceptions of missions and what it means to be a missionary is being re-plotted. I began with an understanding that the mission of God and the work of a missionary were bringing God to a community. While taking a few days away from public ministry, Bishop Mark MacDonald challenged my assumption by saying that "God didn't get off the boat with Christopher Columbus," that is, God was already present and active in North America.[8] With a simple hip check, my assumption was flattened like a hockey player playing with his head down in the corner.

I am beginning to see that the plot isn't about the missionary bringing God to the community. The plot is that the missionary is invited into joining an already active and present God, called to personify grace, mercy, and love. We are all missionaries, called to be little Jesus, if you will, participating in his activity through his body, the church. In a sense, we are all writing another chapter of

---

6. Mark L. MacDonald, interview by author, October 4, 2011. On November 4, 2013, he was elected the North American Regional President for the World Council of Churches.

7. Buster, *Do Story*, kindle loc. 20.

8. MacDonald.

INTRODUCTION

the Acts of the Apostles. Before you get all excited, I'm not suggesting that we add more chapters to the Bible, but that by joining in the redeeming activity of Jesus, the healing activity of the Holy Spirit, and expressing the Father's love, who desires relationship, we are participating in the new creation transformation he has begun.

Being on a mission with an already present and active God transforms one's missionary effort to one of joining the activity of an already present and active God. I don't have to come up with a solution, I do have to identify and participate in the work he is already doing. Leonard Sweet tells the story of coming home to his mother, Mabel Boggs Sweet, always knowing what he and his brothers had been up to. That's part of our responsibility as heirs, to look for signs of God and his dirty, blood-soaked fingerprints. Then we have to testify to what he is up to, encouraging others to join the work he has already begun. This entering into the story with God, from Adam to Jesus, relies, "not on teaching, not on exhortation, not on reason, but on the one human form that can convey truth that we are more than we can ever understand, the only form that is open, the form of pure narrative."[9] There is a great story and we are in it. The work of narrative is shaping our life whether we are aware of it or not; the choices we are making are defining our story. Storytelling and story-catching give us lenses to see our choices within a context that helps us in our decision-making. By giving us a slant, storytelling gives opportunities to view the world and our part in it. Storytelling provides the clarity we seek to seize our destiny, assisting us in understanding that we are not merely victims of someone else's actions; we are called to action, to be protagonists. The biblical narrative invites us to live as protagonists, living into a great story, being formed into a community of God, missionally, relationally, and incarnationally; Leonard Sweet in *So Beautiful: Divine Design for Life and the Church: Missional, Relational, Incarnational,* helped me in unpacking what this all means.

---

9. Josipovici, *The Singer on the Shore,* 23.

Introduction

    A helpful structure that has re-orientated to story-catching and storytelling is understanding that there are two basic types of stories—stories of redemption and stories of transformation. With this story architecture I am able to hear the truth and speak the truth, never denying evil or its capacity with a view towards redemption and transformation. Bad things, evil wicked things, happen every day and often to undeserving or unsuspecting people. It is this desire of redemption from evil, and the hope of evil being transfigured, that helps in understanding evil and the many people who have suffered and/or continue to suffer at the hands of evil. Throughout history many have suffered and experienced the abuse of physical, emotional, and sexual violence, found themselves the targets of crime, witnessing the carnage of accidents, crime, disease, economics, poverty, violence, and the devastating circumstances of genocide, environmental disasters, and war. Yet the world keeps changing; we don't lose hope because stories of redemption and transformation undergird the struggle.

    Understanding that redemption and transformation are the two primary themes of stories, and that all stories have an identifiable structure, has helped me in discovering a whole new way to read, meditate, and understand the story of God that is revealed in Scripture. Through this understanding, I see things that I never saw before. This consciousness of the structure of the story sheds new light on the particulars within the story; each character has a reason for being in the story and often that becomes clear only *as the story unfolds*. The details of place and time are there for context, creating a plausible reality, leaving no doubt that God has what it takes to make it real. This has reinvigorated my preaching and teaching, and strengthened my understanding of how to read, study, and communicate more effectively. Illustrations are no longer the add-ons to the truth, for emphasis, to keep it interesting or to make it easily understood. Stories are the staple, the meat and potatoes, for the narrative of God's redemptive and transformational activity transfiguring the world.[10]

---

    10. It is the practice of this book to use the terms story and narrative interchangeably.

INTRODUCTION

At this point, some of you may be saying, "wait a minute," how did you transition from the people in Saskatchewan who are struggling with their current situations, drowning in addictions, and taking their life as a way of dealing with or escaping their currently desperate situations, to storytelling and the biblical narrative? This book will hopefully help you understand why I have come to this conclusion and how I came to this conclusion. It all began as I started asking myself various versions of this question: Why are people engaging in self-destructive behavior and what is required for them to change? I began with that question because too many people are dying preventable deaths. Having explored several options, my simple answer is that, as one becomes aware of the activity of the present active God, who is love, the possibility for redemption and transformation presents itself as a gift of grace. Discovering one's identity in Christ empowers one to live in and through desperate situations with hope. Semiotically engaging in God's narrative revelation enables one to recognize the activity of God and participate in God's business of restoring and renewing people and places. I have come to this conclusion as the stories of scripture reveal a God who is knowable and wants to be known. This is a God who is love and wants to be loved and we are made to live in relationship with this creator God, each other, and the rest of creation. It is this story of God that offers context and meaning to these relationships. All of the information we receive is given meaning and value by placing it within a narrative construct of our choosing, be that consciously or unconsciously. It is this narrative construct that determines whether information is important, needs to be acted on, ignored, or saved for later.

There are those, like Galen Strawson, who argue that it is "false that everyone stories themselves, and false that it's always a good thing."[11] To which I reply: Have you ever noticed that whenever you buy a car you are surprised by how many cars, like yours, that others drive? Some of you will notice this while you are driving your newly acquired car; perhaps you will begin noticing them while you are considering a purchase. Others of you notice this in

---

11. Strawson, "The Unstoried Life."

Introduction

the parking lot as you're looking for your car and see so many that look alike. We are all different as to what catches our eye. We are all the same in that once we have a context that values something particular, like the car, we pay attention because we have a context—a story that gives them value. What Strawson is objecting to is the notion that any narrative will do, and, as an analytical philosopher and literary critic, he is well positioned to say precisely that. There are narratives that do not encourage truth, beauty, or goodness, and are the antithesis to health. To that point I agree with the objections about the current trend in narrative identity and it is also why, in this book, I invite people not only to live a storied life, but to have an identity formed out of a particular story, a narrative that offers truth in the form of a person, and knowing within the bounds of relationship.

In the following chapters we will take a quick look at the psychological and neurological research that indicates that: (1) healthy brains continually adapt, change, and renew; (2) humans are social, relational storytellers; and (3) the expression of any particular emotion lives out of a particular cultural narrative. This book relies on this research to support the premise that: (1) narrative understanding of identity is both incremental and exponential; (2) all narratives shape meaning and offer identity, but not all narratives promote life and/or health; and (3) the biblical narrative is the key transformational narrative to live out of, offering a redeemed and transfigured identity.

Maybe you are like me and have been at the place where you have understood stories and a narrative understanding of identity as simply artistic license or touchy feely stuff, having nothing to do with the real world or the facts of life. Growing up, I somehow came to the conclusion that, at best, stories were good for fantasy, entertainment, and escapism, and had little to do with what mattered. To think of stories as necessary or essential in identity formation was purely an academic area with interesting arguments or exercises that had no significant effect on my life. What follows is some of what has helped me appreciate the critical role narrative plays in identity formation.

"All our life, so far as it has definite form, is but a mass of habits."

WILLIAM JAMES

Part 1

Narrative Psychology and Neuroscience

HE WAS TEN YEARS old when he started cutting himself. Most of his childhood he bounced between foster homes and the various towns and reserves of his extended family. He had an older sister and two younger brothers, but rarely spent time with them. Everyone thought of him as a problem child. What he knows of his family is that his grandparents were taken from their parents and shipped to a residential school, like freight in a boxcar. It was at this reformatory, disguised as a school, that they were forbidden to speak the language of their forefathers and given white man's haircuts and clothes. Everything that had helped them understand who they were was either taken from them or declared evil. His mother, preoccupied with her own survival, didn't know who his dad was. The only people that paid attention to him were teachers, social workers, principals, police officers, and his mom's angry, drunk boyfriends. In his teens, seeking to be valued, he began spending time with gangsters, drug-dealers, and bartenders; they offered him a sense of belonging and a way of escape. They didn't deny his pain, his toughness, or his value. He confused their selfish valuations for love. This is the way of love and relationships that he learned. It was all about what you could get out of somebody. You

Part 1: Narrative Psychology and Neuroscience

loved them so long as they added value and when they no longer did, they became expendable.

When I met Ben, he had been out of the foster care system for six years. Without a home, he had been living between rehab, girlfriends, odd jobs, and mostly avoiding prison. He tried to keep it together, going to 30-day dry-outs, attending various 12-step groups, participating in court mandated anger management programs, and numerous stints in various skills training programs. This way of living was interspersed with visits to the psych ward, mostly when his ability to cope collapsed, and numerous nights in various drunk tanks. He would do all right for a while, but then a crisis, or a stressor, would trigger him and he would begin his downward spiral once again.

Can Ben ever escape this cycle, isn't this who he is? Is it possible or desirable for him to change who he has become? As we look at the contributions of the neurosciences, logo therapy, narrative psychology, and 12-step programs, we see that they all indicate that change is possible, and often desirable. They all seem to agree that this type of a change requires a narrative understanding of who one is and where one fits in the grand scheme of things: this narrative way opens the door for a dynamic understanding of Christian identity formation.

1

Narrative Psychology

WE ALL HAVE ROUTINES, many that require no attention or explaining, and we follow them as if on autopilot. We follow these practices without any thought or attention; we call these things habits. This morning when you brushed your teeth did you start singing Elmo's song, "Brush, brushy brush, brushy brush brush," or are you more the Barney type, singing, "Oh I'm brushing my teeth on top, it's so much fun I hate to stop,"[1] thinking, gently, circles small, slowly moving around the outside and to the inside? When someone starts telling us about the ordinary, they quickly lose our attention. Yet, when that routine is interrupted, by the unexpected or unimagined—say you chip a tooth—one struggles to make sense of what has transpired and what one has experienced. It is in these unexpected and unimagined situations that people create or alter stories, revising them to make sense of what just happened. It is with stories that we order and find purpose to our lives. Dan McAdams, a pioneer in narrative psychology, suggests that our stories need to be constantly evolving in order to help us make sense of life. The reality is that we are constantly adjusting to include more information and new experiences. It is with the help of these evolving stories that we piece together what may be an

---

1. http://www.bestelectrictoothbrushhub.com/top-3-tooth-brushing-songs-for-children/.

Part 1: Narrative Psychology and Neuroscience

unintelligible assortment of events and experiences, and get some sense of meaning or purpose.

Our stories define how we understand others, the world, and ourselves. Everything that we observe or experience is checked against our existing web of stories. If the story fits we add it to our web of understanding,; if it doesn't fit we try and adjust the story to fit within our web. If the story still doesn't fit we either adjust our web to accommodate this story and sometimes we can't see how it belongs, we either hang-on to it, keeping our options open, or we discard the story. The story of our lives is integral to the development of and understanding of who we are. The story of ourselves, that we tell ourselves, is understood to play a significant and primary role not only in constructing meaning within the context of our experiences but also in determining our emotional health and happiness.

Researchers have developed a test that enables them in twenty questions to determine that "adolescents who report knowing more stories about their familial past show higher levels of emotional well-being, and also higher levels of identity achievement, even when controlling for general level of family functioning."[2] These twenty questions are referred to as the *Do You Know Scale* (DYK). It is an interesting narrative exercise and a great conversation starter with your family and friends. To discover your DYK number you answer the following questions, answering "yes" or "no."

1. Do you know how your parents met?
2. Do you know where your mother grew up?
3. Do you know where your father grew up?
4. Do you know where some of your grandparents grew up?
5. Do you know where some of your grandparents met?
6. Do you know where your parents are married?
7. Do you know what went on when you were being born?

---

2. Fivush, et al., *"Do You Know . . . "*

8. Do you know the source of your name?
9. Do you know some things about what happened when your brothers or sisters were being born?
10. Do you know which person in your family you look most like?
11. Do you know which person in the family you most act like?
12. Do you know some of the illnesses and injuries that your parents experienced when they were younger?
13. Do you know some lessons that your parents learned from good and bad experiences?
14. Do you know some things that happened to your mom and dad when they were in school?
15. Do you know the national background of your family (such as English, German, Russian, etc.)?
16. Do you know some of the jobs that your parents had when they were growing up?
17. Do you know some awards that your parents received when they were young?
18. Do you know the names of the schools your mom went to?
19. Do you know the names of the schools your dad went to?
20. Do you know about the relative whose face "froze" in a grumpy position because he or she did not smile enough?[3]

Your score is determined by the number of questions that you answered yes to. The higher the number, the more likely you are to be emotionally healthy and function out of a known identity, your story.

The narratives that we develop and incorporate shape our understanding of who we are. It is from this raw material of experiences that we construct a story that gives order or makes some sense of our observations and experiences. These stories we craft

3. http://articles.memoriesgrow.com/share/do-you-know-scale-dyk-predictor-of-your-childs-emotional-health-and-happiness.

PART 1: NARRATIVE PSYCHOLOGY AND NEUROSCIENCE

are offering us a way of seeing and understanding life; healthy stories assist individuals in giving unity and purpose to one's life, unhealthy stories lead to despair and death.

Historical Foundations of Narrative Psychology

Victor Frankl observed, while a prisoner in a Nazi concentration camp, that some fared better than others in the tyrannical culture of defeat, and concluded that how one handled these atrocities within their stories enables some, himself included, to continue living with some sense of meaning and purpose, even in the most horrendous of situations. It is out of his experience that Frankl developed *Logotherapy* as a therapeutic tool to assist those in particularly desperate situations in finding meaning and purpose in life. Logothereapy is based on an existential analysis focusing on Kiekegaard's will to meaning.

Elie Wiesel had a completely different experience of Auschwitz and Buchenwald, and his haunting account helped him win the Nobel Peace Prize in 1986. His trilogy *Night, Dawn,* and *Day*, reiterate the importance of knowing your story and the personal devastation that one can experience when one's story is not able to make sense of the evil that one is observing and experiencing. This same desire to help others understand their meaning and purpose led Erik Erickson to coin the term "generativity," which refers to the desire one generation has to help the next. Narrative Psychology grew out of Erikson's work. Michael White and Dan P. McAdams are leaders in the exploration of how our personal narratives lend meaning and purpose to those seeking understanding.

Even though the last thirty years have been labeled the "information age," there is a growing awareness, across the social sciences, that we use stories to make sense of our lives. We appropriate stories and claim them as ours; we change and are changed by the stories that our culture, society, and economy generate. This begins in the early teen years, Erickson highlights, as people begin to construct their own stories to make sense of their life. It is at this time that people begin to understand who they are through these stories of self, establishing a narrative identity. James Fowler, following Piaget stages and Kohlberg stages as a guide, developed a way of understanding the stages of faith development. M. Scott Peck developed a simplified faith development chart based on Erikson's stages outlining the four most common stages.

Interest in the field of narrative psychology began in the 1980s as the disillusionment with personality psychology grew in the late 1960s and early 1970s. By the 1990s, it was a recognizable field of study with new narrative theories gaining momentum. Simultaneously, Dan McAdams observed that, "Scientists in developmental, social, cognitive, clinical, counseling and industrial-organizational psychology became increasingly interested in story concepts and narrative methodologies. Psychotherapists began using narrative therapies."[4] Today, the field of psychology expects a lot from stories, particularly as they relate to a person and their culture. Theodore R. Sarbin may have been correct in 1986 when he proposed narrative as a root metaphor for psychology.

When it comes to one's life, storytelling is not "once upon a time;" it is the serious business of sense making. Recently, Timothy Hoyt has seen that the "narrative conceptualizations of identity hold the promise of integrating Erikson and Erikson's aspects of identity as well as illuminating the processes by which individuals develop identity."[5] This culminating in Rurt Ganzevoot's conclusion, in 2008, that our identity is inseparable from the stories we tell about ourselves.

Literary Foundations of Narrative Psychology

Jerome Bruner, a twentieth-century psychologist, contributed significantly to understanding how stories are used within the context of human lives. Bruner identified two ways of knowing: The *paradigmatic way* and the *narrative way*. The paradigmatic way of knowing is what we learn at school; this is where we learn to

4. McAdams, "The Psychology of Life Stories," 100.
5. Hoyt, "The Development of Narrative Identity in Late Adolescence and Emergent Adulthood," 559.

PART 1: NARRATIVE PSYCHOLOGY AND NEUROSCIENCE

understand rationale, logic, science, and causation. The narrative way of knowing we learn from the stories we hear and tell.[6] Stories that are told of when things don't go as expected, when things deviate from the cultural norms or patterns of behavior, help us with times when things don't go as we expected. Think of the recent news headlines or the stories you heard in the last week. Did they involve people doing what was expected? Most of our headlines, coffee times, and water cooler conversations are typically times when we hear and tell stories of the out of the ordinary or the unexpected. We share these stories because they are interesting to hear and tell. Typically, we are not interested in hearing about what we already know or expect; we want something new. When someone begins telling us what we already know, we cut him or her off, with a summary, "I know," or simply allow our attention to drift, tuning back in when we perceive there is something new.

Narrative is a way of knowing and understanding that is practiced in all cultures and communication: *narrative is transcultural*. Globally, people tell stories to others—socializing. We do not tell stories into a vacuum or simply to ourselves; stories by their very nature are inherently social; stories are developed in a community, for the community. Rubin has observed that, even as one looks at the way people structure the stories about themselves, they mimic the forms of communication we are familiar with, and are inseparable from them. The recollection and recalling of our autobiographical stories is a social act defined by, and defining, a social group.

The stories we construct and tell of ourselves use all the elements of storytelling. We use all the components of storytelling including plots, characters, themes, and tone to express meaning. As we go about this task of establishing and expressing meaning, narrative research has concluded that it is important that we pay particular attention to any recurring or goal orientated ventures or activities in our life story, as they help us understand and identify themes. Donald Miller begins *Storyline 2.0 Conference* by asking participants, "What will the world miss if you don't tell your

6. Bruner, *On Knowing*.

NARRATIVE PSYCHOLOGY

story?"[7] Is there meaning and purpose to your life and, if so, how do you discover it? Or, for those of you more familiar with the paradigmatic way of knowing, Dan McAdams asks this question, "How is a person's psychosocial world arranged in such a way as to provide life with some modicum of unity and purpose?"[8] We can thank Bruner and Polkinghorne for opening the door, in the 1980s, to this way of understanding ourselves, as they proposed that the language of narrative was the best means of addressing these questions.

As we consider the building block of our lives, the highs, the lows, and the times of transition, these are the times that we develop our stories that offer us meaning and identity. It is the stories of our lives, Bauer observes, that enable us "to interpret the past in terms of trait-like perceptions of "who one is" and to plan the future in terms of traits that one wants to continue developing in their lives."[9]

We must remember that our life story does not exist in a vacuum or in isolation; it exists in a community and a culture. Our stories mirror the culture and the community where the stories are birthed and told. Our life story lives in our community and culture. The story of our life is born, grows, reproduces, and dies "according to the norms, rules, and traditions that prevail in a given society, according to a society's implicit understandings of what counts as a tellable story, a tellable life," says McAdams.[10] This, I believe, is one of the reasons that make it clear why living in community with a fellowship of followers of Jesus is so important. We need each other to tell our stories to, since together we figure out what it means to live resurrected lives; we need each other to avoid allowing our pasts to chain our futures. This is why becoming a society dictated by pop culture is so disconcerting. One of the prevailing arguments of today's pop culture is articulated by Macklemore and Ryan Lewis' hit song, "Same Love," when the chorus cries out

---

7. Donald Miller, Storyline 2.0 Conference.
8. McAdams, "Psychology of Life Stories," 114.
9. Bauer, "Narrative Identity and Eudaimonic Well-Being," 92.
10. McAdams, "Psychology of Life Stories," 114.

Part 1: Narrative Psychology and Neuroscience

"And I can't change, even if I tried, even if I wanted to. . . . " The resurrection of Jesus never denies the reality of our birth, or the societal situations and biological conditions of our birth, but says that we should not allow our birth to determine, restrict, or limit our future. The crucifixion and resurrection of Jesus proclaims that change of even the worst possible situation is imaginable, possible, and desirable. In the crucifixion, we see that redemption is offered and in the resurrection we see that transformation is a guarantee.

Philosophical Foundations of Narrative Psychology

Michael White, citing the work of Michael Foucault, traces the roots of the modern internalization of understanding life and identity in Western culture back to the seventeenth century. Dan McAdams, in his research, traces the roots of the Western understanding of identity and life back to as far as the Catholic Fourth Lateran Council, in 1215. This is the council that made the practice of the confessional an annual practice. McAdams notes, in *The Redemptive Self*, that this decision, in 1215, set in motion a social ritual that has affected Western culture's understanding of self and identity in a way that nothing before has, and its effect continues to shape how one thinks about their life. He suggests that, while many in the sciences have viewed the practice of annual confession as manipulative and out of order, in the modern world, McAdams notes that confession can have a profoundly restorative effect on one's narrative identity, particularly in the areas of integrity and wholeness. McAdams, within narrative psychology, sees confession as an act that separates a person's identity from one's behavior, grounding one's identity "in the capacity to keep a particular narrative going."[11] This separation of a problem from a person and their identity, McAdams understands, does not in any way remove the responsibility of the problem from the person or their responsibility to address it. Rather, it empowers the individual to address the problem as a problem and not see the person as the

---

11. McAdams, "Psychology of Life Stories," 111–12.

problem. Problems viewed this way, within the practice of Narrative Psychology, makes it possible for an individual to assume agency, to take an action that produces a desired effect within their story. As long as one sees the person as the problem, there is no hope of having any agency (the capacity to take an action that produces a desired effect) to resolve or address the problem other than to take actions that are self-destructive. This understanding of personhood doesn't seek to deny evil or the effects of sin. What it does seek to acknowledge is that all people are made in the image of God, and that image has been blighted, stained, and tainted by sin. The person bearing the image of God is not the problem, the problem is sin, and the choices sin encourages by its distorted depiction of reality. Sin is distinct from the image of God that all of humanity bears, sin hides and distorts the image of God. Sin is the viral infection of all humanity that is the original and quintessential dis-ease of the image of God bearing humanity. The self is a person made in the image of God, and the problem is the problem—evil is the problem, sin is the problem—not the image of God.

The Practice of Narrative Psychology

Embracing the idea that one is living out of a story means accepting that a personal narrative can be discovered, explored, and developed. As we begin acknowledging that our living is a story-shaped life, there are questions that arise: Are we conscious of our story? Do we see our self with agency in that story? Do we understand that this agency plays out in particular roles, themes, and trajectories within that story? Erik Erickson, in *Childhood and Society*, was the first to identify that we habitually determine meaning and our habits shape who we are. We have an inherent need to make sense of our experiences, to give them coherence. Ordering the events of our life to make sense of them is arguably a central human need. As Laura King observes, "In the face of major life change, human

Part 1: Narrative Psychology and Neuroscience

beings are prone to spontaneously generate stories about what happened."[12]

Generating these stories is not easy; agency in storytelling is multilayered, because the storyteller is giving voice to the story while the main character, the agent or protagonist, of the story "has feelings, beliefs, desires, and identities expressed in interpretive [narrative] content."[13] Marcela Cornejo helpfully suggests that we see our personal histories as one of offering identity; it is a part of who we are that must be dealt with and made sense of if we are to build a narrative understanding of who we are. Our assembling of our history introduces and attempts to give meaning to things that have occurred, the meaning and value we give these events are part of what shapes our understanding of ourselves, who we are, and what role we see ourselves playing.

Twelve-step programs like Narcotics Anonymous (NA), Alcoholics Anonymous (AA), and Al Anon are programs that have assisted many in reconstructing their life stories. One of the central aims of these programs is to assist and support individuals, enabling them to function within society as productive and caring members of a community. But to become aware of this point, participants of the fellowship, addicts, or the person whose life is strongly determined by the actions of an addict, must come to the place of surrender, realizing that they are powerless to effect change, that they need the help of a power outside of them—commonly referred to as a higher power. The philosophical fulcrum of these 12-step programs is that only an external higher power can provide the strength to free one from the contamination of the seductive and deceptive powers of one's addiction or compulsion. One point of contention that I have with 12-step programs is they have no way of acknowledging that a person's story is being or has been reconstructed. A 12-stepper's story must begin with a self-identification of being an addict. "Hi I'm Norbert and I'm an addict." While this is a way of beginning one's story of redemption,

---

12. King, "The Hard Road to the Good Life," 58. See also Pennebaker, *The Secret Life of Pronouns*.

13. Hoyt, "The Development of Narrative Identity," 569.

NARRATIVE PSYCHOLOGY

this in no way recognizes that, for many, a true and lasting transformation has occurred. They are no longer an addict, someone devoted to someone or something habitually or obsessively. Properly speaking, they are someone who was an addict, but they are an addict no more—they have experienced redemption from the destructive obsession and habitual ways, transformed by the renewing of their relationships, choices, and behaviors. As members of the 12-step fellowship are transformed by the strength of a higher power, they insist that the participants continue to identify themselves, first and foremost, by whom they once were rather than what they are. Their addiction, compulsion, or victimization is no longer the identity they function out of, as it is no longer who they are. Many stop going to meetings at this point, as they can no longer, with any integrity, introduce themselves as an addict. Something inside of them screams a denial, "You are not an addict; you once were, but now you're not; you have been and are being redeemed; there has been a change of story; redemption is real and transformation has begun with a restoration of identity." As one is transformed, they are not what they once were; they are changed. The biblical narrative takes it even further and says that we are made new. Isn't this what the Apostle Paul was saying in Ephesians 4:17–24?

> And so I [Paul] insist—and God backs me up on this—that there be no going along with the crowd—the empty-headed, mindless crowd. They've refused for so long to deal with God that they've lost touch not only with God, but with reality itself. They can't think straight anymore. Feeling no pain, they let themselves go in sexual obsession, addicted to every sort of perversion. But that's no life for you. You learned Christ! My assumption is that you have paid careful attention to him, been well instructed in the truth precisely as we have it in Jesus. Since, then, we do not have the excuse of ignorance, everything—and I do mean everything—connected with that old way of life has to go. It's rotten through and through. Get rid of it! And then take on an entirely new way of life—a God-fashioned life, a life renewed from the inside and

working itself into your conduct as God accurately reproduces his character in you. (The Message)

Where is the space to introduce this renewed, God-fashioned life? Should there not be room within the fellowship for; "Hi I'm Norbert, I was an addict but now I'm being made new?" With that, one is acknowledging the redemption that has occurred, while acknowledging the ongoing strengthening of the higher power's transforming work.

The decision to turn to a source outside of oneself for strength and help is acknowledging that a new story is desired, and strength is required to change and begin living out of a new story. For many, this is one of the first conscious acts of agency, acknowledging that their past doesn't have to be their future. This is the beginning of a new story; one is no longer powerless and alone. At this point of the story, it is the reaching outside of oneself to the yet unknown higher power that is important. This can, and needs, to remain open, so as to not erect any barriers. At this point it is perfectly safe to leave it up to the person (the protagonist) to decide who or whom can function as the higher power, and the force or forces of nature that must be reckoned with (the antagonist) in the story.[14] I understand and appreciate the need to be vague in recognizing the higher power that can give strength, but where is the room for the ultimate expression of that strength, in the person being made new? We begin each day anew, creating and finding new daily opportunities for meaning and value. A life story discovered, surrendered, and redeemed—a story with hope and meaning.

The Contribution of Dan McAdams

Less than thirty years ago, all of the sciences, including psychology, considered all stories of an equal value to that of a charming fairy tale. Yes, stories are interesting, perhaps even enchanting, but stories were essentially the realm of children and child's play

---

14. Remembering that it is God, the good Shepherd, who seeks and saves the lost.

NARRATIVE PSYCHOLOGY

compared to the real work of a reasoned understanding of humanity and how one ascertains meaning, value, and purpose. Consider for a moment, do you think all stories are of equal value? Are novels simply the leisure activity of vacations? Or do they play an important part in your everyday life? What stories do you allow to shape your past, present, and future?

Dan McAdams, a leading psychologist in the field of narrative and identity, has developed a life story model of identity that proposes that our understanding of self is found in the elements of a story including the "setting, scenes, character, plot, and theme."[15] This sets McAdams' work apart from the work of Erik Erikson, who understands one's life story as a developmental model of ego identity.

McAdams is not denying that one's identity is formed in adolescence and early adulthood, but argues that the narrative that shapes one's identity keeps evolving throughout the course of one's life. As we live, new events and experiences must be reconciled with our story. We choose to incorporate some of these events into our sense of self and narrative identity, and others we shrug off, suggesting that it has nothing to do with who we are. The life story model that McAdams presents stresses that one's identity is fluid, as one's narrative understanding of self is an ongoing work of assimilating events and experiences into our life's story. McAdams argues that, "Life stories develop and change across the life course, reflecting various on-time and off-time happenings and transitions . . . people may work on different facets or qualities of the story at different times in life."[16] I find this a very helpful way of thinking about identity formation as a way of becoming. Could this be part of what was occurring in the Exodus story, when God redeemed his people from slavery? Calling them out to the wilderness to build a new temple, to reform their community, and to renew their covenant identity as the people of God. Could this be the image John had in mind when he said, "Dear friends, now we are children of God, and what we will be has not yet been

---

15. McAdams, "Psychology of Life Stories," 101.
16. Ibid., 106.

made known. But we know that when Christ appears, we shall be like him, for we shall see him as he is."(1 John 3:2,) We are being transformed, and called out of who we once were, to who we are now—a new creation, a child of God becoming more than we ever asked or imagined.

One's narrative identity development has to do with where one is in one's life, and in culture. For, as we have already discussed, one's cultural setting provides the psychosocial menu out of which we construct our narrative identity. Culture provides the raw material from which one constructs a working narrative identity. McAdams states that our "identity is not an individual achievement but a work of (and in) culture. In a sense, the person and the person's social world coauthor identity. Identity is a psychosocial construction."[17] The work that we do on developing our narrative identity is not merely a personal narrative. As our narrative identity develops within a social and societal context, it says something about who we understand ourselves to be. Our life stories are strongly shaped by our culture; typically what our culture values and finds meaningful, we find meaningful, unless we consciously choose to follow a different narrative that defines meaning differently and gives value by what it defines as meaningful. Our conception of the good life varies from those who live in different cultural contexts. What it means to live the good life is partly determined by our cultural context. Parts of our narrative identity are developed as we assume or adopt stories from our cultural context. Part of the task of our narrative identity is to come to terms with who we understand our selves to be, and the culture that we live in. Never forget the influence of the prevailing cultural narrative's power to shape our stories of redemption and transformation. Our understanding of our narrative expression of self cannot be developed outside of a particular social or cultural context (be they real or imagined) in which they are experienced. This is not a new concept: Moses in Deuteronomy 32 advises Israel to, "Remember the days of old; consider the generations long past. Ask your father and he will tell you, your elders, and they will

---

17. McAdams, "Psychology of Life Stories," 116.

explain to you." Israel had walked out of their story and been subsumed by the cultural norms of their day. Moses is recalling their story, being completely honest about their past and the decisions that have affected them, and says that this does not have to continue. They no longer need to be who they had become; Moses was inviting them to live into their true, but forgotten and abandoned, identity. He tells them to remember the story of who they are, and to live out of that God-given narrative identity. Moses is advising the people of Israel to put into practice every single word of the story of God, concluding that, "Yes. This is no small matter for you; it's your life. In keeping this word you'll have a good and long life in this land that you're crossing the Jordan to possess" (Genesis 32: 47, The Message).

These narrative identities provide the stories with which we choose to live by. We make "and remake them, we tell them and revise them, not so much to arrive at an accurate record of the past, as to create a coherent self that moves forward in life with energy and purpose."[18] McAdams sees human intentionality as being "at the heart of narrative, and therefore the development of intentionality in humans is of prime importance in establishing the mental conditions necessary for storytelling and story comprehension."[19] Story and purpose are inseparable, as they are the two ways that people establish meaning. "There can be no story without intention. Further, there can be no intention without story."[20] As Bauer points out, there is an "empirical connection between certain qualities of narrative identity on the one hand and well-being on the other, it becomes especially important to understand how adults narrate the most difficult experiences in their lives and integrate them into their evolving life stories over time."[21] This is what the work of Dan McAdams seems to revolve around. What McAdams' work does is open the door to change, at any stage of life. The patterns are not set; old dogs can learn new tricks. Or, as the Apostle

18. McAdams, *Redemptive Self,* 98–99.
19. McAdams, "Psychology of Life Stories," 103.
20. King, 58.
21. Bauer, 93.

Part 1: Narrative Psychology and Neuroscience

Paul puts it, "It's in Christ that we find out who we are and what we are living for. Long before we first heard of Christ and got our hopes up, he had his eye on us, had designs for glorious living, part of the overall purpose he is working out in everything and everyone" (Ephesians 1:11, The Message).

The Contribution of Michael White

Another psychologist leading in the field of narrative psychology is Michael White, an Australian, whose contribution to Narrative Psychology is clinically focused. For White, Jerome Bruner's work, *Actual Minds, Possible Worlds*, was a turning point in his narrative practice, as Bruner understood that "great storytelling . . . is about compelling plights that . . . must be set forth with sufficient subjectivity to allow them to be rewritten by the reader, *rewritten so as to allow play for the reader's imagination.*"[22] Duhigg highlights this same point when he suggests that AA "succeeds because it helps alcoholics use the same cue, and get the same reward, but it shifts the routines. Researchers say that AA works because the program forces people to identify the cues and rewards that encourage their alcoholic habits, and then helps them find new behaviors."[23] This reinforces White's observation that sometimes one's life story needs a rewrite and that this rewrite is possible given a new narrative context.

In Narrative Psychology therapy, White views the therapist as one who enables another to re-author one's life. One does this by inviting clients to continue telling stories, and as the stories continue to develop, often helping clients work through particularly "neglected but potentially significant events and experiences that are 'out of phase' with their dominant storylines."[24] It is as these out

---

22. Bruner, *Actual Minds, Possible Worlds*, 35. Emphasis mine.

23. Duhigg, Kindle 1273. For more see Kelly and Meyers, "*Adolescents participation in Alcoholics Anonymous and Narcotics Anonymous*," Journal of Psychoactive Drugs, 259–69 and Kelly, Magill and Lauren, "*How do Peoples Recover from Alcoholic Dependence*," Addiction Research and Theory, 236–59.

24. White, 61.

of phase, or subordinate, stories are redeveloped that clients find ground on which "to proceed to address their predicaments and problems in ways that are in harmony with the precious themes of their lives."[25]

What I find helpful, in terms of identity development and the use of narrative, is that White stresses that the matter of metaphor selection is highly significant. "All metaphors that are taken up in the development of externalizing conversations are borrowed from particular discourses that invoke specific understandings of life and identity."[26] Choosing what metaphors to use is based on what is most viable in the particular situation, given all ethical considerations.

One of the pitfalls of Narrative Psychology that White warns against is the tendency towards totalizing problems in therapy by clients and therapists. Totalizing typically occurs as one becomes totally negative in defining a problem: setting up a false dichotomy, or not living in the paradoxical state of "both" and "and." As we use metaphors, we must be on guard against metaphors that totalize situations or events, as then they function as a suppressant of other metaphors that may be emerging. Part of being semiotically engaged demands that we are able to maintain the tension that keeps agency within the protagonist. I find the guiding metaphor of Crystal Downing's book, *Changing Signs of Truth: A Christian Introduction to the Semiotics of Communication*, helpful in understanding how one lives with this tension. Downing concludes that, "Even though the Holy Spirit joins us on the edge of the coin, as we balance between the Immutable Word and the mutable words, the surface upon which we roll the coin changes with the time."[27] But I'm getting ahead of myself.

White argues that Narrative Psychology can help arouse the curiosity concerning what is possible by playfully engaging the imagination. Just as good stories do not explain everything, or get overly detailed, and invite the reader into participating in

25. Ibid., 128.
26. White, 31.
27. Downing, *Changing Signs of Truth*, Kindle loc. 3000.

PART 1: NARRATIVE PSYCHOLOGY AND NEUROSCIENCE

the story by filling the details of the story, Narrative Psychology therapy helps clients bring together events and experiences from the past, mapping the narrative, assisting the client in recognizing a plot and theme in one's narrative, enabling one to see oneself apart from the problems, and enabling one to see the possibility of redemption and transformation.

Conclusion

Narrative Psychology suggests that our narrative identity is not work done in isolation or in the imagination, but is a collaborative effort of our culture, as well as sharing the narrative within a particular community of listeners. While an identity may not even be contained within a single overarching narrative, it is the narratives that are relied upon to give meaning and purpose within the particular social constructs inhabited, and sometimes we rely on more than a single story to make sense of the varied contexts we live in. The stories and identity of self are not always congruent as if our narrative is separate from our identity; they are distinguishable. The stories we craft give an account of what we perceive has occurred; they provide the context and setting. Each teller of an event has a unique understanding of what occurred, as they make their own connections regarding what was trivial, what was important, why this matters, and how it fits. Every storyteller and story-catcher interprets events according to their perceptions of significance that is uniquely theirs. It is these variables within a story that create and give voice to our uniquely crafted narrative identity. As we proceed through life, striving for a sense of who we are with a continuity of meaning and purpose, we begin to realize that we do this differently at various times for potentially different reasons: ultimately, we are hoping to find the good life.

This look at Narrative Psychology's contribution—to how narrative shapes identity—highlights how the sociocultural context affects an understanding of self. It explored causes and possible courses of restoration for addictions and suicide in a context of broken dreams and economic despair. Despair, addiction, and suicide are not the only ways of escaping desperate conditions. Frankl observes that it is only when there is no narrative context that offers meaning or purpose that life-destroying alternatives appear as viable solutions. Doehring, in *The Practice of Pastoral Care: A Postmodern Approach*, suggests that there are three main issues that people deal with: loss, violence, and compulsion. How these issues are processed and faced is determined by one's understanding of self and the story they see themselves participating in. The cycle of despair and destruction continues as long as the problems are understood as internal problems within the person. This is not a denial of the doctrine of original sin; sin is real and everyone is born into sin, bearing the marks of a sin-stained life. People are not made for sin, but are marked by sin. All are born bearing a sin-stained image of God; and it is this sin-stained-image-of-God-bearing person that Christ loves, forgives, redeems, restores, and transforms. All of humanity is born with a sin-soiled image of God. When the person is the problem, the problem is solved by the elimination of the person. Conversely, if the problem is exclusively outside of the person, it can be avoided as a non-issue, having nothing to do with the person and requiring no personal action. To realize that you have agency means that you realize that your choices matter and change the future. Your past does not need to determine or rule today, or tomorrow. Once we acknowledge that we have agency, we can decide what actions define who we are. With this agency comes the realization that we are protagonists (a significant character in our story). Having separated the person from the problem, we are able to address the problem without eliminating the person.

In addressing these problems, we may realize that we are encountering an antagonist, "a higher power," that is not against us, but can empower us to change. The problems are not what define who we are; the problem is what defines our choices, as we are the protagonists. As we begin to see ourselves as protagonists, with intrinsic value and worth, we begin drawing breaths of hope. The worth of a person is not tied to their economic valuation, social status, or political affiliation. God's revealed narrative offers us a provenance—a history that establishes that we belong, and have inherent value and intrinsic worth. In the Scriptures, we are drawn into a story of belonging to the family of God. Out of love we have been created in the image of God. We are sinners, invited to be God's beloved children in every way imaginable—forgiven, invited, and encouraged to call God, the highest power, our Father.

Many have lost their place in this story, or do not see that this is their story. Pope Francis recently said it well when he was asked who Jorge Mario Bergoglio is? "I do not know what might be the most fitting description . . . I am a sinner. This is the most accurate definition. It is not a figure of speech, a literary genre . . . the best summary, the one that comes more from the inside and I feel most true is this: I am a sinner whom the Lord has looked upon."[28]

Placing our understanding of narrative identity within a theological metaphor, Origen's metaphor of provenance is helpful. Origen explains that *Logos* is not only the original painting. *Logos* is the artist painting, and the human soul is like a reproduction. Because God is the painter, the image cannot be destroyed; it can only be buried or obscured. Our decisions and activities brush many different colors on the image, painting over the image with every imaginable brush stroke of sin. But as one turns towards God, one allows God (the highest power) to become the great restorer, removing all color, dirt, and soot that has distorted the image made.

Understanding that problems and challenges are outside of our self is often difficult. Remembering that the original beauty is still present may be even more difficult to imagine. We are image bearers of God and it is this identity that makes the entire endeavor of restoration possible. We bear the image of the truth, beauty, and goodness of a God who is present and active in the here and now. We may not see or know him, we may not even understand, appreciate, or realize it, but he is the God who is with us. It is God with us that rips off the veil of despair and death; resurrection has happened, restoration and transformation is happening, and all things are being made new. (Romans 6, 7:6, 1 Peter 1:18)

28. Spadaro, "A Big Heart Open to God."

Narrative Psychology

In researching Narrative Psychology, I can see that, as we begin to understand our story and identity within the context of *Logos*, we can have hope for things not yet seen and possibly previously unimagined (Hebrews 11:1–13). For when our *imago dei* is restored, there comes a point when the once-soiled painting no longer sees or refers to itself out of its old, soiled identity. There comes a point when one no longer sees himself or herself as an addict, but as a sinner who is being redeemed and restored as a child of God. I have and am witnessing this. Hurting people are being redeemed and restored and some of them no longer can identify themselves as an addict, since that is no longer a part of their story, it is who they were (1 Cor. 6:11). By the grace of God, the sociocultural context has enabled followers of Jesus to write "addict" completely out of their narrative identity.

Hopefully, this brief look at Narrative Psychology will help you to live as a sinner, redeemed by grace and participating in the story of God, who is already present and active, walking with friends and companions who are in various phases of *Logos* restoration. "Every one of us is unworthy to stand and confess to being a disciple. Every one of us loves and lives this reality of brokenness. But the good news is this: God uses broken things."[29]

---

29. Sweet, *Strong in the Broken Places*, 9–10.

2

Neuroscience

EARLIER, WE LOOKED AT Jenny, who dropped out of college, returned to her tribal village, and a year later she was pregnant and infected with HIV. While Jenny's story is fictional, many in northern Saskatchewan would see it as their story, or have points of connection with this story. Charles Darwin, Ayn Rand, Frederick Nietzsche, and others see little cause for concern since they promote that it has always been about the survival of the fittest, and the fittest determining the story. Ayn Rand, in *For the New Intellectual*, gives voice to this attitude in Galt's speech: "To help a man who has no virtues, to help him on the ground of his own suffering as such, to accept his faults, his need, as a claim, is to accept the mortgage of a zero on your values."[1] Others like Brian Boyd see our stories as forms "of cognitive play . . . a playground for the mind."[2] What role does our mind or brain play when we think of stories and identity?

Do we dare to bring a hard science, such as neuroscience, into the conversation of narrative identity formation? Isn't the realm of story one of the last sacred preserves of our imagination, untouched by the Enlightenment? Should we not protect stories like we try and protect the wilderness and endangered species? Should

1. Rand, *For the New Intellectual*, 180.
2. Gottschall, *The Storytelling Animal*, 43–44.

story not be the one place science does not penetrate, with science fiction given a necessary literary exemption, of course? Are we willing to allow the realm of the story to be conquered by science, reducing the ancient mysteries to an electrochemical function? There are even those who say that the challenge of neuroscience, in trying to understand how the brain works, is like trying to understand how a bird flies by looking at a feather. Not to mention that our current cultural tendency is, as Allissa Quart observes in *The New York Times*, to allow neurological explanations to "eclipse historical, political, economic, literary and journalistic interpretations of experience."[3] Somewhere along the way, we have forgotten that life and its story are about the interplay between form and history.

Storytelling involves assessing the symptoms, diagnosing the problem, and then shaping healing. Almost every good story, throughout the ages, has followed this three-act structural pattern, where the story is about a protagonist's journey to secure, usually at some cost, what they desire. Story = Character + Predicament + Transubstantiation.[4] That there is a three-act pattern should not disturb, surprise, or cause concern, as Michael Shermer states, "There is now substantial evidence from cognitive neuroscience that humans readily find patterns and impart agency to them."[5] The conclusion seems to be that we as humans are pattern seeking by nature. Shermer identifies this pattern making as "agenticity: the tendency to infuse patterns with meaning, intention, and agency."[6] Michael Gazzaniga in his research has "identified specialized circuitry in the left hemisphere that is responsible for making sense of the torrent of information that the brain is always receiving from the environment. The job of this set of neural networks is to detect order and meaning in that flow, and to organize it into a coherent account of a person's experience—into a story."[7]

3. Quart, "Neuroscience under Attack."
4. Buster, *Epiphany: How Understanding Story Creates Change.*
5. Shermer, *The Believing Brain*, 88.
6. Shermer, 87.
7. Gottschall, 96.

Part 1: Narrative Psychology and Neuroscience

Bruce Hood documents "the growing body of data that demonstrates our tendency not only to infuse patterns with intention and agency, but also to believe that objects, animals, and people contain an essence—something that is at the core of their being that makes them what they are—and that this essence may be transmitted from objects to people, and from people to people." Hood goes on to say that "many highly educated and intelligent individuals experience a powerful sense that there are patterns, forces, energies, and entities operating in the world. . . . More importantly, such evidence is not substantiated by a body of reliable evidence, which is why they are *super*-natural and unscientific. The inclination or sense that they may be real is our supersense."[8]

This also helps us understand the conclusions David Aaronovitch reaches about conspiratorial thinking when he states that our obsession with conspiracy theories "is a reflex of the storytelling mind's compulsive need for meaningful experience."[9] Conspiracy theories offer ultimate answers to a great mystery of the human condition: why are things so bad in the world? "They provide nothing less than a solution to the problem of evil . . . [bad things] happen because bad men live to stalk our happiness. And you can fight, and possibly even defeat, bad men. If you can read the hidden story."[10]

We prefer to receive and share knowledge with stories because we, by nature, are story-catchers and storytellers. Stories assist us in making sense of the world and what we are experiencing and observing. We like our stories to have distinct structures, with clear beginnings and ends, and we usually like things to happen for particular reasons that progress in sequence. We are just beginning to understand what priests and shamans have known for quite a long time, as message worked into a story burrows into our minds.

8. Shermer, 88.
9. Gottschall, 116, referring to Aaronovitch, *Voodoo Histories*.
10. Ibid. Barkun in *A Culture of Conspiracy* has done some interesting work on conspiracy theories and where they originate.

Neuroscience

Neuroscience is concluding that humans are distinct. We are not like the rest of the animals that are social creatures. As humans, we not only create a social order—we have the capacity for this social order to take on an institutional reality. This is a uniquely human behavior. John Seale explains that this institutional reality develops to form an organization that is concerned with obligations and permission. It is this system of obligation and permission that gives us an essential component with which to organize our society, giving us the "capacity to create and act on desire independent of reasons for action."[11]

Neurological research is coming to the conclusion that stories not only stimulate our brains; stories have the ability to change our behavior. In reviewing brain scans, typically done using fMRIs,[12] neuroscientists have discovered that something unexpected happens when we read an evocative metaphor, a detailed description, or an emotional exchange between characters.

> A team of researchers from Emory University reported . . . that when subjects in their laboratory read a metaphor involving texture, the sensory cortex, responsible for perceiving texture through touch, became active. Metaphors like "The singer had a velvet voice" and "he had leathery hands" roused the sensory cortex, while phrases matched for meaning, like "the singer had a pleasing voice" and "he had strong hands," did not.[13]

These findings help demonstrate that our neural networks store information as "a pattern of activation across networks of neurons. . . . In the neural networks that process language and meaning, the pattern representing the word you believe you

---

11. Searle, *Freedom and Neurobiology*, 109.

12. *f*MRI stands for Functional Magnetic Resonance Imaging. It is a functional neuroimaging procedure using MRI technology to detect blood flow changes within the brain to ascertain brain activity. Connecting cerebral blood flow with neuronal activity does this; therefore, as blood flow to a region increases, brain activity increases. This has become the preferred and dominant method of neurological research since the early 1990s, as it is the least invasive for observing brain function.

13. Searle, 109.

Part 1: Narrative Psychology and Neuroscience

encountered was triggered as part of the collateral activity of all the other words that were processed and encoded."[14] Murphy Paul, in her *New York Times* article "Your Brain on Fiction," concludes that our brains hardly differentiate "between reading about an experience and encountering it in real life; in each case, the same neurological regions are stimulated."

This function relies on our memory of previous experiences; it is our memory that ceaselessly places us:

> Between a thoroughly lived past and an anticipated future, perpetually buffeted between the spent yesterdays and the tomorrows that are nothing but possibilities. The future pulls us forward, from a distant vanishing point, and gives us the will to continue the voyage in the present. This may be what T. S. Elliot meant when he wrote: "Time past and time future / what might have been and what has been / Point to one end, which is always present."[15]

Or, as Robert Beelah puts it, "no past, no future: it's that simple. One might also say, no present either."[16]

We need the memories of our past, and our anticipated futures, to live. Abuse and trauma research suggests that there are forms of trauma that can be stored in the primitive portions of our brains, tattooing the trauma onto our memory. How do we figure out what to remember of the past when there is no possible way anyone could remember everything about their past, and yet there are some things we cannot seem to forget. How does our memory work? Munsterberg's theory of memory proposes that while, "none of us can retain in memory the vast quantity of details we are confronted with at any moment in our lives and that our memory mistakes have a common origin: They are all artifacts of the techniques our minds employ to fill the inevitable gaps."[17]

---

14. Hood, *The Self Illusion*, 80. Referring to Roediger III and McDermott, "Tricks of Memory,," 123–27.

15. Damasio, *Self Comes to Mind*, 297.

16. Bellah, *Religion in Human Evolution*, Kindle 35.

17. Mlodinow, *Subliminal*, 61.

Neuroscience

Leonard Mlodinow believes that we remember and "perceive by engagement, rather than by passive receptivity, ... [that is] the reason why we often recall contexts rather than just isolated things."[18]

No one believes that they can remember everything. Forgetting is commonly accepted, and it seems to be expected that one forgets as they age, but to get to the point where we realize that what we remember is a fabrication of our story-making brain desiring order is something else. Once we begin to wrestle with this, it begins to make us question everything that we call to mind or think we remember. This means that we can remember things and events in living color that never, ever happened. This realization has the ability to completely destabilize any notions of trust in what we think we remember, removing the confidence we typically place on our memory.

Perhaps, Hood is right in saying that memories are "stories we retrieve from the compost heap that is our long term memory; we construct these stories to make sense of the events we have experienced."[19] We tell ourselves stories, as our mind seems to be adverse to coincidences, uncertainty, and randomness. Our minds are habituated to finding meaning. When we cannot find meaning or identify meaningful patterns, we struggle to adapt and find meaning. We simply cannot live with disorder, even if we think we can. When things or events occur that do not make sense or fit our established patterns, we do our best to fit them into patterns. Then, when no pattern works, we are confronted with the need to create a new way of ordering that attempts to make sense of our reality or experience, whether this re-ordering is true or not. As humans we need some way to accept the memories of our past, or find a way to live with and through them.

James Wallis writes that, "Our brains have a natural affinity not only for enjoying narratives, but learning from them, but

---

18. Damasio, 133.
19. Hood, 221. Randall is credited with the metaphor for one's memory as "a compost heap in a constant state of reorganization." Randall, "From Compost to Computer: Rethinking our Metaphors for Memory," *Theory Psychology*, 611–633.

also for creating them. In the same way that your mind sees an abstract pattern and resolves it into a face, your imagination sees a pattern of events and resolves it into a story."[20] Bellah concurs with this when he says that he was learning more about himself and the world that he lives in and these stories were shaping his understanding. "After all, that's what stories do."[21]

There is more to stories shaping our understanding than what appears on the *f*MRI. Since the beginning of psychology, von Helmholt, Freud, and others saw that there were processes that we were not conscious of that determine our decisions and actions. What is now being realized "is the extent to which these processes are there to protect the self illusion—the narrative we create that we are the ones making the decisions."[22] To be able to look at the whole of the human experience and begin to understand it, we must address and engage both the conscious mind and the unconscious mind. Our unconscious mind "influences our conscious experience of the world in the most fundamental of ways: how we view ourselves and others, the meaning we attach to everyday events of our lives, [and] our ability to make quick judgment calls and decisions."[23] We have to address the idea of free will and realize that while the "experience of free will is very compelling, and even those of us who think it is an illusion, find that we cannot in practice act on the presupposition that it is an illusion."[24]

As we seek to understand the formation of the conscious and unconscious mind, we must acknowledge that, when compared to all the other creatures, human adolescence and childhood takes a disproportionate amount of our life. Antonio Damasio suggests that the reason for "the inordinate amount of time is because it takes a long, long time to educate the non-conscious processes of our brain and to create, within that non-conscious brain space, a form of control that can, more or less faithfully, operate according

20. Gottschall, 104.
21. Bellah, Kindle 909.
22. Hood, 156.
23. Mlodinow, 5.
24. Seale, 43.

to the conscious intentions and goals."[25] Stories shape our unconscious and conscious mind and "help us practice key skills of human social life. They also provide a basis to run fictional simulations in our head and hearts. See a movie, read a text, participate in an action; in all of these events we activate bodily representations of what it feels like."[26] Our brains take our bodies through the actions required, imagined or real.

Lev Kuleshov, in his film experimenting with un-narrated images, demonstrates how unwilling we are to be without a story. The "Kuleshov" effect shows how we interpret images and put a story to them to make sense of what we see. Gottschall mentions a more recent study where a group was asked to choose a pair of socks out of seven pairs of identically priced socks. As people explained their choices, they referred to texture, color, and quality, even though the seven pairs were identical. The real pattern that no participant was able to identify was that they tended to choose from the right side of the display. Everyone created a story to explain their choice but "the stories were confabulations—lies honestly told."[27]

Add to that our natural inclination to order and create stories, and we come up with reasons for why we did what we did, or chose what we chose. As a consequence of this, Kathryn Schultz writes, in *Being Wrong*, that, "To know what we don't know, we can't just passively wait around to see if our mind comes up empty. Instead we need to actively identify and reject all the incorrect and ill-grounded hypotheses our inner writer is madly generating."[28] She states that the real problem with being wrong is that it feels exactly like being right. Our natural default is to rely on our stories that create order, whether they are true or not.

Not being able to differentiate between a coherent and an incoherent story, or having an inadequate story, is what often leads to depression, according to Michele Crossley's research. Our personal identity resides in the story we tell our self and so does our

25. Damasio, 271.
26. Gottschall, 57 63.
27. Gottschall, 106-10.
28. Schultz, *Being Wrong*, 82.

Part 1: Narrative Psychology and Neuroscience

social identity. As Robert Bellah states, "Families, nations, [and] religions know who they are by the stories they tell."[29] As Damasio states:

> There is indeed a self, but it is a process, not a thing, and the process is present at all times when we are presumed to be conscious. We can consider the self-process from two vantage points. One is the vantage point of an observer appreciating a dynamic object—the dynamic object constituted by certain workings of minds, certain traits of behavior and a certain history of life. The other vantage point is that of the self as a knower, the process that gives a focus to our experiences and eventually lets us reflect on those experiences.[30]

We return to Jenny and her story. Unfortunately, Jenny's story has failed her and her peers have enforced her failure—welcoming her into their story of despair. It is the only story presented that enables her to order her experience. She, like all of us, instinctively reaches for a meaningful story to help her understand and interpret the world, even if those stories are of hopelessness and despair. Jenny has lost, forgotten, or given up on stories worth believing in and adopting. For her, the stories she is believing in and adopting no longer require what is true, good, and beautiful, they lack the ability to hold these three components in a dynamic tension, offering hope. It is true, as Hood says, that, "Who we are is a story of our self—a constructed narrative that our brain creates."[31] The stories we allow to order and create our story are the stories that draw us into understanding who we are. When the story draws us in, all of our rational, logical defenses are dropped. We are moved by our emotions, leaving us vulnerable and defenseless against the influence of the story. Once our emotions and beliefs are embraced, our brain seeks evidence that will confirm our experience. This

---

29. Bellah, 771.

30. Damasio, 34. Palmer, *To Know As We Are Known*, and Buber, *I and Thou*, are two works that address the self and the other, wrestling with where they meet.

31. Hood, xiii.

Neuroscience

then gives an emotional boost that encourages our confidence in our beliefs, as Shermer notes, accelerating the process of reinforcement, "round and round the process goes in a positive feedback loop of belief confirmation."[32] Jenny's story of an anticipated future has been replaced with a story of despair and hopelessness.

In order to effect any change towards hope, Damasio suggests that Jenny needs to become aware of the deliberate and conscious decisions she has made in facing her failure. It is only as she does this that she will be able to discover her unconscious decisions that determine her conscious attitudes and actions. "One way to transpose the hurdle would be the intense conscious rehearsal of the procedures and actions we wish to see non consciously realized, a process of repeated practice that results in mastering a performing skill, a consciously composed psychological action program gone underground."[33]

If we have learned anything from interpersonal or social neurobiology, it is "that the brain is constantly rewiring itself based on daily life. In the end, what we pay the most attention to is what defines us. How you choose to spend the irreplaceable hours of your life literally transforms you."[34] Michael Shermer goes on to explain that:

> We form our beliefs for a variety of subjective, personal, emotional and psychological reasons in the context of environments created by family, colleagues, culture and society at large; after forming our beliefs we then defend, justify, and rationalize them with a host of intellectual reasons, cogent arguments, and rational explanations. Beliefs come first, explanation for beliefs follow. I call this process belief dependent realism, where our perceptions about reality are dependent on the beliefs that we hold about it. Reality exists independent of human minds, but

---

32. Shermer, 5.
33. Damasio, 281.
34. Ackerman, "The Brain on Love. See James K.A. Smith, You Are What You Love."

Part 1: Narrative Psychology and Neuroscience

our understanding of it depends upon the beliefs we hold at any given time.[35]

It is true, neuroscience has observed, that it is our brains that "make us do it," but this in no way excuses our personal responsibility for our actions. Jenny adapts to her new situation as she copies or mimics, this most powerful of skills that we are born with.[36] Not only do we have a natural inclination to mimic, we have smoother interactions with and tend to like strangers who mimic our mannerisms. As Jenny finds acceptance, mimicking behavior, and her peers accept her; then the more she becomes accepted by her peers, the more she mimics the behavior that made her acceptable in this group to begin with, and the spiral of descent into despair begins.

Jenny's understanding of her current status changes how she remembers her story, just as children's memories are "aided by parents reminiscing with their children."[37] Jenny becomes a different person as her story changes and as she spends time with her new acquaintances. Cooley suggests this most strongly when he "argued that no real identity exists separately from the one created by others. We are a product of those around us—or at least what we believe they expect of us."[38] "The memories we recall to define our self story are defined by the groups to which we belong."[39] After analyzing 86 fMRI studies, Raymon Mar indicates that:

> A substantial overlap in the brain networks used to understand stories and the networks used to navigate interactions with other individuals—in particular, interactions in which we're trying to figure out the thoughts and feelings of others. . . . Narrative offers a unique opportunity to engage this capacity, as we identify with characters' longing and frustrations, guess at their

35. Shermer, 5.
36. Hood, 61, referring to Meltzoff, et al., "Foundations for a New Science of Learning," 284–88.
37. Hood, 241.
38. Ibid., 72, referring to Cooley, *Human Nature and the Social Order*.
39. Ibid., 241.

hidden motives and track their encounters with friends and enemies, neighbors and lovers.[40]

This highlights that the stories Jenny is allowing to shape her identity are altering who she understands herself to be, as well as restructuring her memories of successes and failures.

Neuroscientists, in the last few years, have come to realize that stories engage and activate more parts of the brain than initially expected, offering a plausible explanation as to "why the experience of reading can feel so alive. Words like 'lavender,' 'cinnamon' and 'soap,' for example, elicit a response not only from the language-processing areas of our brain, but also those devoted to dealing with smells."[41] Narrative has the ability and capacity to refashion our identity as it reaches into our body. Story with all of its power to transform contains a womb, full of conceptual possibilities.

The present becomes bearable as our story begins to fashion a hope that the power to change is accessible. "A sense of purpose doesn't come from thinking about it. It comes from taking action that moves you toward the future. The moment you do this, you activate a force more powerful than the desire to avoid pain."[42]

Shermer ends his book with the statement, "In the end I want to believe. I also want to know. The truth is out there, and although it may be difficult to find, science is the best tool we have for uncovering it."[43] I find his conclusion odd and inconsistent, as neuroscience seems to be pointing towards story as being the way to truth.

Brian Boyd may be more right than many care to admit, that we are living "in a world awash with junk story," and this leads to "something like a 'mental diabetes epidemic.'"[44] Perhaps, by asking neuroscience for definitive explanations, we are asking for an

---

40. Paul, "Your Brain on Fiction."
41. Ibid.
42. Stutz and Michels, *The Tools*, 33.
43. Shermer, 344.
44. Gottschall, 198.

Part 1: Narrative Psychology and Neuroscience

answer that it is not able to provide. Growing up, we are told, "it is only a story." Everything in us tries to believe this; all of the efforts of science and education try to reinforce it. But, as adults, we must return to our childhood way of knowing, where we see "that the story has its own truth that such disclaimers don't reach."[45] The question is: what narrative will you choose to address the biggest stuff in human life? We need to see patterns in our past to make paths for our memories, so that we can shape our present and future. Like Jenny, we all need our social influences to verify and validate our story.

In northern Saskatchewan there is an epidemic of "junk stories." Jenny provides a prototypical example of what it is like to live with a loss of meaning and purpose, where the infection of "mental diabetes" is rampant. Addictions and unhealthy lifestyle choices are symptomatic of this loss of story. For Jenny, her failed attempt was seen as the end, when that is not what it should have been. What is needed is a story with room for failure, like the story that enabled Thomas Edison to see failure as a thousand ways that would not work. Edison said once that, "I haven't failed. I am not discouraged, because every wrong attempt discarded is another step forward."

"A sense of purpose doesn't come from thinking about it. It comes from taking action that moves you toward the future. The moment you do this, you activate a force more powerful than the desire to avoid pain."[46] Neuroscience has led us to the altar of story. Story is how we order and understand our experiences and give them meaning.

Hopefully this overview of some of neuroscience's recent conclusions has strengthened your understanding of the role and purpose of story in identity formation—discipleship. With any luck it may have encouraged you to keep catching and telling the story of God's revelation found in the Bible. Even Gottschall agrees that the Bible is "a collection of intense narratives about the biggest

---

45. Bellah, 752.
46. Stutz and Michels, 33.

stuff in human life."[47] Why is it that we, in the church, have missed this?

The presentation of these findings are meant to fan the flames of interest in telling God's story in a manner that allows people to not only see the change, but to live into the change, as participation changes our identity. This research leads me to conclude that merely knowing the story and seeing how it works is not enough. We need to be able to read our self into the story. To do this we need to be able to recognize the activity, the signs and symbols, of the living, active God, which is the role of theo-semiotics. I am beginning to see that our narrative identity formation is a core discipleship practice that is ongoing. Seeing also that narrative identity formation offers a way of hope in places of despair and hopelessness, offering a gift, enabling and equipping others to choose a new story to live out of. This narrative identity formation, in terms of discipleship, may be understood as a "narraphoric" way of following God. A narrative understanding of Christian identity formation prepares one to face the varied challenges of life, equipping one to face disillusionment and the reality of evil, offering hope in the most forlorn situations.

---

47. Gottschall, 117.

One cannot make a new heaven and a new earth with facts.

HENRY MILLER

Part 2

Story Matters

AFTER IT HAPPENED, I knew what I should have done, but didn't do. Let's be honest, I couldn't do it anyways. I was a failure. Riddled with guilt and shame, I withdrew. What did it matter anyway? I knew the right answers; I could talk a stranger through it, yet nothing changed. Life was passing me by as I sat on the bleachers of life. I was a spectator. I could tell you what they were up to; one liked sailing and the other had a passion for Africa. Just don't ask me what I was doing; it didn't seem significant or important, especially since I knew what others were doing to change the world and bring healing and hope to this broken world.

Then one day, it was as if I was called from the bleachers to play. It wasn't that there wasn't anyone else. He picked me, drawing me in for something that he had uniquely prepared me for. Not despite, or because of, my failures, but because he loved me, seeing that my brokenness was where he could build strength. My history mattered to Him; He gave me a new way to see my story, changing everything.

I'm reminded of the tale from India that Mary Dressein tells of a water-bearer who carried two large pots on a yoke across his shoulders up the hill from the river to his master's house. One pot was cracked and leaking, the other always delivered a full pot of water from the river. After years of arriving half-empty, the cracked pot apologized. "I'm sorry that I couldn't accomplish what the perfect pot did." The water-bearer replied, "What do you have to apologize for?" "All this time, I delivered half my load of water. I make more work for you because of my flaw." The water-bearer smiled and said, "Take note of all the lovely flowers growing on the side of the path where I carried you. The flowers grew so lovely because of the water you leaked. There are no flowers on the perfect pot's side."

3

Why Story

WE CURRENTLY LIVE IN a culture of cynicism, where one is taught to disbelieve what one hears and to be skeptical of what one sees and reads. We trust what our friends tell us and what we tell our self. In making this observation, Seth Godin comes to the conclusion that it is the role of a leader to "give people stories they can tell themselves."[1] Everyone needs stories, for it is through stories that we get to know who we are and how we fit in. Facts without a narrative are irrelevant bits of binary code, all ones and zeros. As we place the things we see, hear, taste, touch, and experience into a narrative construct (a story) we begin to grasp at meaning and purpose, as bits and bytes are connected, written into a code, operating in a relational context.

Our identity depends on stories, and it is through stories that we understand who we are. It is from stories that we learn and interpret the meaning making of self and others. But how does this story-catching, story-crafting, and story-telling happen? Brian Boyd observes that what we, as humans, do is take the massive amounts of information we receive, quickly and unconsciously running it through a pattern recognition sieve, incorporating the information as best we can with the sieves we have, and making

1. Godin, *Tribes,* 138. See also Timothy Martin, "Illuminating the Landscape of Religious Narrative," 393.

PART 2: STORY MATTERS

new pattern sieves as required to sort the information we receive. Through this sorting, by pattern recognition, we see shapes and share gathered facts in a manner that reflects the patterns of sense making we know, as there is a continual intake of bits and bytes. This pattern-seeking nature of humans enables us to quickly assimilate facts, as it is this pursuit of pattern making that enable us to "yield the richest inferences to our minds."[2] Stories give a context and add meaning to our ideas, observations, and experiences.

The ability to tell stories is central to problem solving, according to the work of Tim Brown and Barry Kātz. Stephen Denning champions the notion that it is through stories that the shared values of a community are transmitted, and it is through stories that common meanings are established. Denning writes about how stories enable "communities to see the world differently, to experience the internal 'ah-ha' that revitalizes and reframes how they connect with each other and the world."[3] As Kate Marek notes, one is informed, persuaded, enlightened, connected, and moved through stories.

Brian Boyd introduces *On the Origin of Stories* with an understanding that one needs stories to provide a context for decision-making. According to Boyd, it is stories that provide "clues to the present, hints from the past, examples or analogies for reasoning about the future."[4] Stories help one to remember the past, so that one can re-member the present, and the future. This remembering requires us to use our imagination, for it is with our imagination that the stage is set for the story to unfold. Our imaginations are essential, for it is the fuel empowering "narrative, tradition and practice [to] perform their dance," notes Diane Butler Bass.[5] The imaginative use of stories helps us to live into a freedom that our current reality may not reflect. Stories provide a context that al-

2. Boyd, *On the Origin of Stories*, 14.
3. Denning, *The Leader's Guide to Storytelling*, 156.
4. Boyd, 167.
5. Bass, *The Practicing Congregation*, 98. Two important books on the theological significance of the imagination are Green, *Imagining God* and Bryant, *Faith and the Play of Imagination*.

Why Story

lows us to explore possibilities of how our current situation can be understood, redeemed, and transformed. As we learn to imagine possibilities, with ease and a sense of play, it can make the difference between despair and hope, fear and courage. Good stories engage us honestly with a sense of uncritical playfulness that lend a sense of courage and hope for the future.

Whether we acknowledge it or not, everyone lives within a story. I know there are some, like Galen Strawson, who challenge the entire concept of a narrative self, saying that it is false that we can attribute control to self. Preferring to believe that, while narrative may be helpful for some, it doesn't apply to all. While I disagree, he does draw attention to some of the dangers of self storying, perhaps even arguing for the need for a narrative beyond and outside of oneself, within which to find ones own story. His quarrel seems to hinge on how we answer the questions—is one conscious of their narrative and does one need to be in order to have a true understanding of self? To which I would say that it is common to be unaware of the story we are living in, and even when there is an awareness of having a story, by inattention, distraction, or unintentionally one can find that they have wandered out of their story. Forgetting our history can also lead to losing a sense of personal identity and membership in a community. We need to cling to narratives because they assist in remembering who we are. It is in the stories and traditions we remember and practice that our understanding of personal and community identity is embodied. Without a particular story to differentiate humanity, what makes humanity different and unique from the other creatures? Sometimes I even think our lack of a story or narrative understanding of ourselves is our story, or at least it was a part of who I am as I to am relatively new to this way of seeing.

Stroup offers words of caution for when we find that we are "no longer part of a community that is struggling to appropriate its stories and traditions we run the risk of losing that memory that binds us to others, both in the present and previous generations."[6] It is not uncommon for communities to struggle with their history;

6. Stroup, 431.

everyone has regrets concerning their behavior or what they have witnessed. When you lose the understanding that you are part of a larger story, you lose the ability to remember your history. Stroup suggests that North America's fascination with story "suggests a crisis of memory in the social fabric;"[7] a crisis that one desires release and relief from.

The loss of story in culture is indicated by a personal and corporate failure of imagination. Wendell Berry, in *Imagination in Place*, says that: "Though you may get a new life, you can't get a new past. You don't get to leave your story. If you leave your story, then how you left your story is your story, and you better not forget it."[8] Berry suggests that you cannot or should not try to escape or deny your past; if you do, your story becomes a story of denial and escapism. Living out of a story that does not deny one's past requires an imagination, for without an imagination one cannot live creatively.

It is in the realm of the biblical narrative that one's imagination is stirred, inviting the possibility of new paradigms of redemption and transformation. Our stories must give meaning and purpose to our experiences, these stories must address all areas of experience and observation: body, soul, mind, and spirit. Good stories do not avoid the past or gloss over present realities; they factor in the unabridged events and experiences of our life. Good stories enter the diversity and complexity of life, respecting the diversity and differences while searching for meaning in the complexity by remaining open to patterns as they present themselves.

This desire for redemption or reinvention is not uncommon; according to Ann Rice and F. Scott Fitzgerald, they are the only two themes in all of literature. It is this desire for redemption and reinvention, or transformation, which should define the mission of the Church. Robert Jensen sees the core task of the church to be one of telling "the biblical narrative to the world in proclamation and to God in worship, and to do so in a fashion appropriate to the content of the narrative; that is, as a promise claimed from

7. Ibid.
8. Berry, 91.

Why Story

God and proclaimed to the world."[9] Chapter 5 and 6 of the book of Joshua provide a good example of just such a narrative. Christ is promised, Christ has come, Christ has died, Christ is risen, Christ will come again, is what the Church is to be about. While Jensen does not include "Christ is promised" in his summary of the Gospel, there is a growing awareness of anticipation of Jesus within the Old Testament among biblical scholars. It is this story of promises being fulfilled, where redemption and transformation are being realized, that the church needs to portray in word and deed, offering hope to a world longing to be found in a story that makes a difference.[10]

---

9. Jensen, "How the World Lost its Story," 31.

10. Sweet and Viola, *Jesus: A Theography*. For more on unpacking the soteriology implications see Wright, *After You Believe* and Geoffrey Wainwright, *Doxology* for more on the doxological import.

4

Culture

IN THE WORLD THAT was modernity, it was assumed that one lived in a "narratable world," where stories could be shared that were authentic to it. As Jensen says, in modernity it was understood "that the reason narratives can be true to the world is that the world somehow 'has' its own story, antecedent to, and enabling of the stories we tell about ourselves in it."[1] Boyd helps us see how stories depended on an understanding of events and the sequencing of those events before we place them within a narrative. He goes on to say that narrative in modernity depended on the "capacity for Meta representation: not only to make and understand representations but also to understand them as representations."[2] But we can no longer assume to begin by asking, do "you know the story you think you must be living out in the real world? We are here to tell you about its turning point and outcome . . . [When] the church does not find her hearers antecedently inhabiting a 'narratable' world, then the church must herself be that world."[3] I understand that part of what Jensen is getting at is that we can no longer begin conversations with, "you are a sinner; let me tell you how to be forgiven." As there is little narrative context of sin, there is little

1. Jenson, 33.
2. Boyd, 129.
3. Jenson, 34.

need for understanding the need for forgiveness; but if we, as the church, inhabit a place in the community that practices redemption and transformation, it once again becomes a story others wish to become a part of.

The power of the story must be released; the remembering must begin. It has been forgotten that Jesus was a storyteller who engaged people by telling stories. As Don Miller points out, "nowhere in Scripture does God step in and say now here is the point. . . . The point is the story itself."[4]

In a TGIF's (Twitter, Google, Instagram, Facebook, Snapchat) environment, we need to offer a storied world back to the world, and one of the ways we do this is by acknowledging that everyone can tell stories. It is with social and mobile media that many are telling their stories and trying to make sense of the world that they live in. Annette Simons, in *Whoever Tells the Best Story Wins*, observes that many are floating "in an ocean of data and disconnected facts that overwhelms them with choice. . . . In this ocean of choice, a meaningful choice—a meaningful story—can feel like a life preserver that tethers us to something safe, important, or at the very least more solid than disembodied voices begging for attention."[5] The Gospel, like any momentous story, is a story that requires a narrative world. "If the church is not herself a real, substantial, living world to which the gospel can be true, faith is simply impossible."[6] One begins by acknowledging that the twenty-first century belongs to those who will tell the best stories. It is in the story arts that people are finding a way of imagining how to live their life and these stories are shaping many of today's dreams and expectations. But this will be no easy task. Paul Auster points out that:

---

4. Miller, "How Narrative Shapes Culture," lecture, April 2007. This does not deny that the narrator of a story provides interpretation of the truth; the narrator helps tell the story so one understands what occurred in the story, otherwise the story catcher may miss an important detail within the story.

5. Simmons, *Whoever Tells the Best Story Wins*, 5. For more on overwhelming choice see Schwartz, *The Paradox of Choice*.

6. Jensen, 34.

PART 2: STORY MATTERS

The prospect of building congruent, life-giving narratives in this day and age, however, are highly debated. Postmodern theorists like Jean-Francois Lyotard argue that the "master narratives" that shaped the modern, Enlightenment society—like historical progress, the rational self, and the enlightenment science—have ordered or collapsed. Parallel changes in religion—like the decline in biblical literacy, authority, and confessional traditions—confirm that the "grand narratives" of denominations and congregational life no longer hold the power they once did. Because these master, framing narratives are week or missing, people are bombarded by an endless stream of images, vignettes, and emotional moments in this postmodern culture, to the point that many become "saturated selves" without agency or purpose.[7]

Kenneth Gergen highlights this crisis of "saturated selves" because the biblical narrative has fallen silent, and with no story to remember we forget who we are. This saturated selves dilemma leaves us with an uneducated imagination, scrambling to find a narrative or god that can help us make sense. Northrup Fry, in his little book, *The Educated Imagination,* concludes that stories do not reflect life and neither do they escape or withdraw from life: "It swallows it. And the imagination won't stop until it's swallowed everything. No matter what direction we start off in, the signposts . . . always keep pointing the same way, to a world where nothing is outside the human imagination."[8]

The pursuit of our rational obsession has led the modern church to give up on the storied imagination as the way of knowing truth, as there is no way of reconciling the paradox. The reality of God must be presented and proclaimed in terms of narrative, for that is the way God chose to prepare for and reveal the Incarnation to humanity. Eberhard Jungel states this in a very helpful way; "If thinking wants to think God, then it must endeavor to

---

7. Goleman, "Reclaiming the Story," *Congregations,* 8. Quoting from Auster, *The Locked Room.* See also, Lyotard, *The Postmodern Condition.*

8. Frye, *The Educated Imagination,* 33.

tell stories."⁹ A return to storycatching and storytelling that places us within the paradoxical stories of God's activity of redemption and transformation is needed to offer our world a space where the possibility of hope can be grasped. That is why this book focuses on the role of narrative in identity formation, the biblical narrative must be allowed to play a key role in Christian identity and faith formation.

9. Jungel, *God as the Mystery of the World*, 303.

5

What is a Story?

WITH AN ARGUMENT FOR the stories presented, it will be helpful to define what it is that we mean by referring to stories or narratives. There are a variety of definitions that spring to mind, yet, simply understood, a story is the arrangement that orders and gives meaning and significance to information. Stories contain plots, themes, characters, change, and locations. In understanding story, it is helpful to agree with Polkinghorne that narrative and story, in the broadest everyday sense, are synonyms.[1] When thinking about stories, it is important not to restrict oneself to the use of words, as narratives are not dependent on the exclusive use of words. As Boyd suggests, a narrative "can be expressed through mime, dance, wordless picture books or movies."[2] In fact, a story "gains impact through enactment or the emotional focusing that music offers in dance, theatre, opera, or film or the visual focusing in stage lighting, comics or films."[3]

While we primarily depend on language to express ideas and concerns, there are a variety of tools used to communicate these ideas and concerns. Yet, the communication of ideas in

1. Denning, *The Secret Language of Leadership*, 229. See also Hoffman, 235, and Denning, *Leader's Guide*, xxiii—xxiv. .
2. Boyd, 130–31.
3. Ibid., 159.

What is a Story?

conversations and speeches provides information—they are not stories. Stories have a power that is unique to them—they can open wallets and spur hearts, minds, and feet into action, moving people in the direction of the storyteller. By their very nature, a trace of strategy will always be discernable in stories. As Denning has outlined:

> The most effective stories usually include: The story of what the change is, often seen through the eyes of some typical characters who will be affected by the change. The story of how the change will be implemented, showing in simple steps how we will get from "here" to "there," and the story of why the change will work, showing the underlying casual mechanisms that make the change virtually inevitable.[4]

Stories involve change—change that has happened, change that needs to happen, and change that can happen.

As Bobette Buster observes, all successful films tell one of three stories: Cautionary tales, stories of fear faced and overcome (redemption), or stories of finding the courage to become fully alive (transubstantiation). Perhaps, Josipovich is headed in the right direction when he:

> Places narrative above theology, reality above consolation. It does seem so, to me, because it recognizes that in the end the only thing that can truly heal and console us is not the voice of consolation but the voice of reality. That is the way the world is, it says, neither fair nor equitable. What are you going to do about it? How are you going to live so as to be contended and fulfilled? And it contains no answers, only shows us various forms of response to these questions. And from Adam to Jesus it is constant in its reliance not on teaching, not on exhortation, not on reason, but on the human form that we convey the truth that we are more than we can ever understand, the only form that is open, the form of pure narrative.[5]

---

4. Denning, *Secret Language*, 36.
5. Jocipovici, 23.

Part 2: Story Matters

We are all part of a community—members tied together by our stories. It is the act of telling honest stories, and participating in the rituals of these stories, that we become community. Healing becomes possible as the trauma and pain we remember is shadowed and salved by a larger storied world that we live in. This is why the biblical narrative is so critical for Christian identity formation—we are a people invited into participating in the story of redemption, restoration, and transformation. We are, as Tom Wright puts it, a people "being remade, judged and remolded by the spirit" through the biblical narrative.[6]

As we ask questions regarding our identity, who am I, why me, what am I here for? I suggest that we need to ask: what do stories offer? How do stories assist with these big questions? What is it that we need to know to live well? We need to know many things for a variety of reasons. Wendell Berry writes that:

> For the time being, and say that we need to know who we are, where we are and what we must do to live. These questions do not refer to a discreet category of knowledge. We are not likely to be able to answer one of them without answering the other two. And all three must be answered well before we can answer with a further practical question. . . . How can we live without destroying the sources of our life?[7]

He continues saying that, with a story, "you reach for reality inaccessible merely to observation or perception but that also requires imagination, for imagination knows more than the eye sees, and inspiration, which you can only hope and pray for."[8] Stories offer clarity without oversimplifying. Stories express human character and the revelation of that character in crisis and stress-filled situations.

---

6. Wright "How Can The Bible Be Authoritative."
7. Berry, *The Way of Ignorance*, 59.
8. Ibid., 50.

6

What Kind of Stories?

OUR TWENTY-FIRST-CENTURY WORLD NO longer lives in the "realistic narrative" world of Jane Austen, Edward Gibbon, and James Baldwin or, for that matter, our local newspaper or soap opera. The modern way of telling a sequence of events is characterized by the notion that:

> Sequential events are understood jointly to make a certain kind of sense—a dramatic kind of sense. Aristotle provides the classical specification of a dramatically coherent narrative. In a dramatically good story, he said, each decisive event is unpredictable until it happens, but immediately upon taking place is seen to be exactly what "had" to happen. So, to take the example of Aristotle's own favorite good story, we could not know in advance that Oedipus would bind himself, but, once he has done it, instantly see that the whole story must lead to and flow from just this act. Second, the sequential dramatic coherence is of a sort that could "really" happen . . . with this kind of narrative, the question of whether the story depicts something beyond itself, and if it does how accurately, are therefore subsequent and independent questions.[1]

---

1. Jensen, 32–33.

Part 2: Story Matters

As Denning writes, we live in a time where the most effective stories "do not necessarily follow the rules laid down in Aristotle's *Poetics*. They often reflect a different tradition in storytelling, in a minimalist fashion, which is reflected in the parables of the Bible."[2] We live in a world where stories are told, liked, commented on, and shared in the Twitter, Google, Instagram, Facebook, and Snapchat narrative realm; it is in this realm that today's world is making known its passions and imaginations.

Additionally we live in an age that has a fluidity of voices. Timothy Martin doesn't see this fluidity as a cacophony of confusion, but as a time of opportunity for the choosing of "religious stories and narrative forms that appeal to the cultural life-world of the students offer even greater potency for a 'fusion of horizons.'"[3] ABC's television series *Once Upon A Time* is a popular example of how this fusion of horizons is practiced—fusing the distant world of fairy tales with a fictional place of Storybrook, Maine, 2011. These "fusion" stories function as stories always have, striving to inspire and encourage people, living here in this place at this time, for what lies ahead.

To demonstrate the value of a narratable world, Herbert Anderson tells of what occurred in the early 90s when a women psychologist was brought to a refugee camp, in Tanzania, to address the women's inability to sleep:

> The women, who had witnessed unspeakable atrocities, had been told not speak of the rape and slaughter they had seen. Memories of the horrors haunted them, and they could not sleep. In response to the situation, the psychologist created a story tree—a place of safety where the women could speak of their experiences. Every morning, the psychologist went to the edge of the refugee camp and waited under the huge canopy of the shade tree. The first day no one came. On the second day one woman appeared and told her story and left. The next day another came, and then another, and another; within the span of a week, scores of women were gathering under the shade

2. Denning, *Leader's Guide*, xvii.
3. Martin, "Illuminating the Landscape of Religious Narrative," 394.

What Kind of Stories?

tree each morning to listen and share their terrifying tales of violence and death. Finally after weeks of the ritual of the story tree, it was reported that the women were sleeping.[4]

We need stories to give voice to otherwise unspeakable suffering. We need rituals to express "what cannot be captured in words. They make the invisible visible."[5] Storytelling practices are "a vehicle for liberating us from narratives that confine and for retelling stories that liberate. We tell meaning laden stories with our lips; we also perform them with our bodies in ritual form."[6]

You cannot move culture unless you move its heart. If redemption or transformation is to occur, "They [the hearers] have to discover it for themselves in the form of a new story."[7] This is what has stirred me to evaluate how evangelism and discipleship is practiced in the twenty-first century. For it is not merely a new story that is generated, it is a credible story to live by that is capable of being lived into, and lends understanding to life.

> The newly emerging narrative is constructed both from the ongoing stories of the people and their organization, and from the new story put forward by the leader. It is born in the listeners mind as a more compelling version of their ongoing life stories. The listeners themselves create the story. Since it is their own story, they tend to embrace it. What the leader says is mere scaffolding, a scaffolding to a creative process going on inside the listeners.[8]

When I read this I felt that Denning had torn a page out of Jesus' narrative playbook and appropriated it. We in the Church need to live into the Gospel narrative, allowing a more compelling version of our life to be born out of the new story put forward by Jesus, the Christ. The question never was: were you born, or

---

4. Anderson, 42.
5. Ibid.
6. Ibid.
7. Denning, *Secret Language*, 34.
8. Ibid., 35.

will you die, but how did you live? As William Wallace says, in the movie *Braveheart*, facing execution, "All men die. But not all men truly live."(Matthew 25:31-46) As the story of life unfolds, each character has the opportunity to practice a sense of purpose, participating in the action. "It will be convincing but not overwhelmed with unnecessary detail. It will include plenty of detail to ground it to some plausible reality. It will leave the audience with no doubt that the organization narrating it has what it takes to make it real. All this takes skill and imagination."[9]

This is the kind of story that engages the mind, touches the heart, and inspires hope. In creating stories, we are participating in the possibility of a different future, even if the story is about the past or a future that we may desire to be a part of, even if one cannot imagine participating in it.

---

9. Brown and Kātz, 137.

*The rich tapestry of human life certainly bears witness
to the variety of ways the good life exists.
Although happiness may be one important thread,
the fabric of life is more than silk and spun gold.
Surely, bad days and bad times are part of the good life.*

LAURA KING

Part 3

Artisan's of Identity

OUR COMMON RESPONSIBILITY AS humans is "to imagine [a] humanity the heart can recognize."[1] To do this we must acknowledge that global culture of the twenty-first century is returning to orality, using the language of narrative and metaphor. We have to let go of our stranglehold on the biblical story, insisting that there is only one right way to tell the story. In narrative, we unearth a toolbox filled with tools, each devised for a particular purpose, yet suitable for use in many circumstances of yesterday, today, and tomorrow. As we use these specifically designed devices in different circumstances and experiences, a beautiful narrative tapestry is woven.

What I am encouraging is more than simply a call for stories, better communication, or a re-ordering of information, but a narrative intelligence that encourages a whole new way of looking at things. We must learn to live with the ambiguity that our stories and other people's stories cannot be completely known or told. By entering a narrative way of knowing, we are living into the great story, where our worrying is defused, and in doing this we release others and ourselves from simply living instrumentally.

Story provides the framework giving structure and meaning in a demanding and changing culture. It is a good story that offers

1. Berry, *Way of Ignorance*, 85.

meaning and context to the givenness of life; narrative makes it possible to accept and be released from our past; it gives purpose and strength to our present, no matter what the circumstances are, and offers hope for the future. Narrative allows one simply to be.

And this is the exact opposite of the place where we left Jenny as she was struggling to make sense of her experience, wondering what the point is of continuing. But Jenny's story does not end here, nor is this simply her finding a new story that gives her meaning and purpose, and she lives happily ever after. This is no fairy tale; this is real life. Come summer, with her belly beginning to bulge, a few of the older women in the community begin befriending her. As she began listening to their stories, she learns of their failures and the struggles they faced. Her new story is beginning; with their encouragement, she begins going to NA, not for herself but for her unborn child. She's working through the steps, discovering that someone outside of her cares and gives her the strength to stay clean.

7

Biblical Story

THE MASSIVE SUCCESS OF the *Harry Potter* and *Lord of the Rings* franchises demonstrates the enduring power of a story, well told, that explores the limits beyond rationalism. Eugene Peterson, when speaking of the centrality of story, observes that the North American Church does not know what to do with these stories, or really any stories. As we get acquainted with this language that comes in the form of story, we do not "know exactly what is going to take place or who it will let in, or how it will end. . . . A story is not a script to be copied,"[1] nor is the ending to be manipulated or controlled by the protagonists, and that is difficult to accept, especially using the leadership and programmatic models popular in many churches today.

Yet, this submitting to the story does not nullify the importance of endings, particularly happy endings, but places them outside the sphere of the protagonist. Happy endings are not fantasy, or escapist, or fugitive, nor do they "deny the existence of *dycatastrophe*, of sorrow and failure; the possibility of these is necessary to the joy of deliverance;" says J. R. R. Tolkien. He continues to say that happy endings deny "universal final defeat, and in so far is *evangclism*, giving a fleeting glimpse of joy, joy beyond the walls of the world, poignant as grief. . . . When the sudden 'turn' comes

1. Peterson, *The Pastor*, 118.

we get a glimpse of joy, and heart's desire, that for a moment passes outside the frame, rends indeed the very web of the story, and lets a gleam come through."[2]

It is this gleam that makes stories so influential, taking the particular and breathing life into it, even in our contemporary postmodern environment. We easily forget that postmodernism is not anti-modernism, but rather a perspective that maintains a greater degree of openness to the mysterious or unexplainable, that is neither naïve or gullible. As Le Grys argues, now "is time to challenge the modernist [rationalist] stranglehold on factual models of the Bible, and allow Scripture once again to tease the mind."[3]

But how does one enter the biblical narrative so that it becomes one's story? Miroslav Volf, in *Exclusion and Embrace*, tells of the time when Jürgen Moltman asked him, at the conclusion of his lecture on loving your enemy, "Can you embrace a *cetnik*?" As Volf struggled to answer, "what would justify the embrace? Where would I draw the strength for it? What would it do to my identity as a human being and as a Croat?" Volf knew what he wanted to say. "No, I cannot, but as a follower of Christ I think I should be able to."[4] How does one become able to? How does one allow God's story to shape one's identity, becoming a lover of one's enemy? Or, how does one begin to permit the Biblical narrative to function as a transformational narrative?

One can begin by allowing the sun to set on reading the Bible as a Rorschach inkblot, where one projects one's own values and ideas onto the Bible; "instead of being swept away into the Bible's story, Rorschach thinkers sweep the Bible into their own story. Instead of being an opportunity for redemption, the Bible becomes an opportunity for narcissism." Scot McKnight continues, saying

---

2. Tolkien *Tree and Leaf,* 68–70.

3. Le Grys, *Shaped by God's Story,* 123.

4. Volf, *Exclusion and Embrace,* 9. A *cetnik*, a variant spelling of Chetnik, refers to a Serb nationalist and monarchist paramilitary organization. Croat refers to a South Slavic ethnic group whose homeland includes Croatia, Bosnia and Herzegovina.

that, "Reading the Bible becomes patting ourselves on the back and finding our story in the Bible, instead of finding the Bible's story to be our story. Instead of entering into that story, we manipulate the story so it enters into our story."[5] This is a dangerous situation indeed as this displaces the God of the biblical narrative, thereby divesting the narrative of its transformational power, turning the narrative into a pragmatic how-to manual.

---

5. McKnight, *Blue Parakeet*, 49.

8

The Story of Self

As we look at the biblical narrative whole, Scot McKnight warns that we must guard against a functional pragmatic approach that is characterized by a stripping of the narrative of the first two (Genesis 1 and 2) and the last two (Revelation 21 and 22) chapters of the story, effectually, having the story begin in sin and end in judgment, instead of revealing the story that goes from good to good (from engagement to consummation).[1] Within the creation narrative, one learns the story of one's life as one is drawn into a way of understanding one's identity and life: an understanding that acknowledges the vulnerability of humanity being the only creature given a garden for sustenance, and clothes to cover one's nakedness. To deny this vulnerability is to deny one's image-bearing, sin-scarred identity. Humanity's vulnerability and interdependence has led to the majority of conflicts within and beyond the Biblical narrative. Yet it is this hostility that makes the biblical narrative so great, as great stories are told in conflict. To embrace the potential greatness of a story requires that we not resist the conflict that we find our self in. One resists by refusing to identify God as unjust, as this causes a distortion and disorientation within the narrative arc. Instead, one starts by embracing God as a master

---

1. Ibid., *The King Jesus Gospel*.

The Story of Self

storyteller, who can be trusted as just and merciful.[2] He is the one who created the garden for man and he is the one who gives life to man by his breath. We must establish the dynamic tension of the Bible where, on the one hand, "it is all about us" and, on the other, "thou art dust and to dust shalt thou return."

As one hears of this God-shaped, God-breathed life, one is introduced to an understanding of man's breathing as breathing God's breath: as *pneuma* is breath, one "cannot not breathe, [one] cannot not pray."[3] If one begins with the creation narrative's understanding of man as one made in the image of God, one is able to appreciate God's Spirit as life-sustaining breath. Thomas Altizer, continuing this thought, says that one needs to declare his name, to name oneself. "For the God whom we have been given has named Himself in us, and named himself in such a manner that we cannot dissociate His identity from our own."[4] Recognizing with Michael Foucault that man made in the image of God is by necessity a "theological conception." This image of God-bestowed identity opens one to a world charged with possibilities, giving man an identity (*imago Dei*) and a vocation (to conserve and create) gratified by the activity of God. Being "created in the image of God, the human subject reflects divine subjectivity. The self-conscious individual reflects the self-conscious God."[5] Echoing Buber's assertion, "I become through my relation to the Thou,"[6] that declares one knows and is known in relationship.

A relationship characterized by the seeking of the best interest of the other is dynamic and fluid, almost synergistic. Having a relational understanding of God allows us to relate to God as someone with whom we can have a relationship with, for God is Emmanuel—God with us. A relationship with books and words, even words that evoke our emotions and inspire our imaginations,

---

2. Miller, *A Million Miles in a Thousand Years*, 31.

3. Peterson, "*Prayer*," Lecture Series, *Practices*. For more on "cannot not love," see Yong, *Spirit of Love*.

4. Altizer, *The Descent into Hell*, 37.

5. Taylor, *Erring*, 40.

6. Buber, *I and Thou*, 11.

is limited by its ability to be reciprocal and symbiotic. There is little capacity for affinity with words compared to the affinity we have with God whose image we bear. For God is much more than words printed on onion skins and dressed in leather, he is the God who is before, above and beyond the Bible—Word made flesh. The Bible unleashes the story-filled self-revelation of God to humanity; revealing a God who is madly in love with his creation, desiring to be loved, and not venerated as an object or seen as an institution to be sustained. As we have conversations with those whom we are in relationship with, we take time and keep attention, and we are changed. These life-giving, life-changing relationships grow trust as we tend to each other, and as that trust grows honesty and intimacy flowers. In this caring of the other we reveal ourselves, running from our self-perceptions, leading to a flight one to another. This enabling one to enter God's story, his-story, of human life, as we truly have everything that we need when we have each other. The reality is that, as Miller says, "if the character doesn't change, the story hasn't happened yet."[7] We cannot assume that we are living a storied life unless we are witnessing change in our life and change around us. The two necessary elements for engaging in a storied life are that "the thing a character wants must be difficult to attain. The more difficult the better." And "the ambition has to be sacrificial. The protagonist has to be going through pain, risking his very life, for the sake of somebody else."[8]

Thinking in terms of story means thinking in terms of change and character development. One begins to realize, with Charlotte Gordon and many others, that the biblical characters, particularly those of the Old Testament, have populated imaginations for centuries, and while never denying their imperfections, religious practices, or desires, these protagonists are part of how one measures oneself. As one aspires to understand who one is, and why one strives for particular dreams, or why is it that one prefers some things to other things that cause strong adverse reactions, one needs to engage the stories of the Bible.

7. Miller, *A Million Miles*, 68.
8. Ibid., 156.

The Story of Self

When looking at the Biblical narrative, it is helpful to remember that:

> A historian might guide you on a search for the "real" Abraham, Sarah, and Hagar, and help you explore the actualities (the socio-economics, diet, customs, marriage practices, etc.) of the people of the second millennium BCE, the period when these figures lived. A theologian could help you uncover many of the religious meanings of this story, its impact on your faith, and your view of God. With an archeologist, you might get to go on a tour of the ancient sites and look for the evidence that these peoples, or people like them, existed. And, finally a Bible scholar could help you understand when this story might have been written down and the politics and historical stratagems that helped shaped the narratives.[9]

The difficulty is that these professions keep the text in the hands of experts. While these professions are helpful and informative as to the nature, context, and meaning of the text, they remove the story from its *primary objective of revealing God with his people*. For some it seems an impossible task, as all these professions lock the text into what was, leaving one with a "that was then" understanding, and shedding little light on how one lives into the story today. The transformational character of the biblical text requires the present, active tense. A challenge that almost seems impossible as Kevin Kelly asks, how can one "restore a 2,000-year-old religion so that it no longer rejects, no longer chases, but actually leads a modern, pluralistic culture running at the speed of Twitter?"[10] That is the challenge one faces when reading the biblical narrative as a transformational narrative. Bonheoffer is helpful in wrestling with this as he sees the Revelation placing the "I into truth," seeing it as "a contingent occurrence which can only be welcomed or rejected in its positivity—that is to say, received as a reality—but not elicited from speculations about human existence as such."[11]

---

9. Gordon, *The Woman Who Named God*, xvi.
10. Lyons and Herbst, *The Next Christians*, dust jacket.
11. Bonheoffer, *Act and Being*, 80.

Part 3: Artisan's of Identity

This professionalization of the text has removed the essential character or story questions from the hands of the reader. Nonprofessional readers are not encouraged to ask: "Who were these characters as individuals? Why did they do what they did? Did they change over time? What do[es] the Bible . . . suggest about their personalities, strengths, and flaws?"[12] Robert Alter, a respected advocate of the biblical narrative, concludes *The Art of Biblical Narrative* by inviting us into a biblical narrative where the authors take "delight in the artful limning of these lifelike characters and actions, and so created an unexhaustable source of delight for a hundred generations of readers. . . . That pleasure of imaginative play is deeply interfused with a sense of great spiritual urgency." The biblical characters are complicated, often alluring, often fiercely insisting on their individuality; it is in this "stubbornness of human individuality that each man and woman encounters God or ignores Him, responds to or resists Him." The paradoxical truth may "be that by learning to enjoy the biblical stories more fully as stories, we shall also come to see more clearly what they mean to tell us about God, man and the perilously momentous realm of history."[13]

What has happened to the biblical narrative Ralph Underwood likens to the "squiggle game" devised by Winicott to assist his work with children. Winicott would draw a few lines on a piece of paper that had no particular meaning, and the child would be asked to take over and complete the drawing. The initial squiggle came from the unconscious, but in the response made by the child, and through conversation that accompanied the exercise, both participants would negotiate meaning in the drawing as their relationship developed. The meaning that emerges from a seemingly random event is thus multidimensional; it is certainly a response to the squiggles, but it is also a response that evolves through negotiation. While it is not a free for all, because the initial squabble imposes constraints on the possibilities or development, there might even be agreed social constraints, in that some versions of the game

---

12. Gordon, xvi, xvii.
13. Alter, *The Art of Biblical Narrative*, 189.

begin with an agreement between both participants about a set of ground rules. Even so, each response displays both "intentionality and creativity." Underwood suggests that any biblical text taunts a reader with "what are you going to do with me?"[14] Gordon states that, "It is our responsibility to seek out this book [the Bible] and reevaluate who we are in relationship to the past. Otherwise we are left with an inert document of apparently contradictory messages that antagonists can deploy, mining the text for one new weapon after another, defending arguments of hate."[15]

One needs to begin to understand oneself as a protagonist in the text, living in a world full of meaning. Our language is pregnant, carrying a range of meaning based on history and expectations. Gadamer argues that tradition plays a large role in determining meaning, making tradition and social context partners in meaning making. But since the crafting of our story is an ongoing process, our preconceived notions continually evolve as we strive to continue to make sense of ongoing events, thus completing the circle of a living tradition.[16]

What I am encouraging is to come to the place where words matter, simply because words flow out of people. Alan Jacobs, in *A Theology of Reading*, formulates a theory of reading where he makes these two important observations:

1. Written words are personal communication from one person to another; and,
2. The proper relationship of a Christian to a person's communication is to love that person by listening to their words.

Listening is an art form not often considered when thinking about reading or love, but as Klyne Snodgrass points out, even in Scripture the biggest complaint "is that people do not listen to God. Theirs is a freely chosen deafness." Choosing not to listen contradicts the *Shema*, "*Hear* O Israel . . . Love the Lord your

---

14. Le Grys, 113.
15. Gordon, xvii.
16. Gadamer, *Truth and Method*, 268–310.

God"(Deuteronomy 6:4–5). Snodgrass, in his article "Reading to Hear" in *Horizon in Biblical Theology*, reaches this insightful conclusion: Israel is commanded to love God, but, before they are commanded to love, they are charged to hear. Jacobs extends this notion of listening and loving in his hermeneutic of love to include not only living persons, but also includes the books and authors of the Bible as neighbors. In effect, this brings the old, old story into the present. Treating these authors and books as neighbors involves listening to them and hearing the challenge of the common contemporary assumption of our identity, of who is in charge. The Biblical narrative clearly draws us into a story of participation where we are not in charge—the Triune God is.

9

A Biblical Imagination

WHEN WE READ THE story of King David and Bathsheba, we are alarmed at the double moral failure of a great king. How could he? Robert Alter, in *The David Story*, points out that this decline is anticipated several chapters earlier, and this incident is the finale of David getting completely out of touch with who he is in the sight of God. The story is about what happens when one believes that they are the worshiped one. The biblical narrative always tells the story of how mankind is designed to flourish as a worshipper. Donald Miller makes the same point when he says that, "The main way we learn story is not through movies or books; it's through each other. You become like the people you interact with."[1] Our passions and desires are shaped by stories. What one values and sees as important is determined by the stories that have permeated one's life. One lives into the stories one has absorbed.

For too long one has been deceived by a rationalist account that says one can think for oneself, assuming "one is what one thinks." But sociological, psychological, and anthropological research does not seem to support the rationalist premise that it is thinking that initiates action. There is a growing body of research indicating that it is one's primed/storied orientation to the world that initiates action. One needs to be captured imaginatively, but

1. Miller, *A Million Miles*, 160.

Part 3: Artisan's of Identity

how does one capture the imagination? As James K. A. Smith said at a lecture I attended, "We live at the nexus of body and story; we are narrative animals." One needs to accept that, "The gospel is a design project and worship is the design studio . . . Liturgies are tactile stories that capture our imagination."[2] In other words, we become what we worship.

Stories help one to not only recall the past, but also assist one in imagining a different future, a new direction.[3] If we are to develop a biblical, personal narrative, one must also develop a hopeful imagination, seeing the world with fresh eyes. Miller describes this imaginative world as being in that place where "God sat over the dark nothing." He put us explicitly in the story "with the sunset, and the rainstorm as though to say, enjoy your place in my story. The beauty of it means you matter, and you can create within it even as I have created you."[4] Resonating with that is what C. S. Lewis said in response to why he wrote the *Chronicles of Narnia* and *Perelandra*:

> I wrote fairy tales because the Fairy Tale seemed the ideal Form for the stuff I had to say. Then of course the Man in me began to have his turn. I thought I saw how stories of this kind steal past a certain inhibition, which had paralyzed much of my own religion in childhood. Why did one find it so hard to feel as one was told one ought to feel about God or about the suffering Christ? I thought that the chief reason was that one was told one ought to. An obligation to feel can freeze feelings. And reverence itself did harm. The whole subject was associated with lowered voices; almost as if it were something medical. But supposing that by casting all these things into an imaginary world, stripping them of their stained glass and Sunday school associations, one could make them for the first time appear in their real potency? Could one

---

2. Smith, "Imagining the Kingdom," lecture. For more on narrative animals see, Smith, *Desiring the Kingdom*, and Brooks, *The Social Animal*.

3. Doerrer-Peacock, *Space, Symbol, and Story*, 17.

4. Miller, *Million Miles*, 59.

not thus steal past those watchful dragons? I thought one could.[5]

One develops an imagination to get over one's conscious and unconscious constraints. It is only as one begins to live imaginatively into one's own story that one can see that, "The whole point of the story is the character arc. You didn't think joy could change a person, did you? Joy is what you feel when the conflict is over. But it is the conflict that changes the person."[6] Or if one prefers more traditional language, "'Being in Christ' means the possession of the new direction of will."[7] It is as one takes the hope-filled, determined, and imaginative posture of Job and stops expecting God to put an end to all of life's troubles that one can be truly surprised at how spending time with God is something you want to do. That Jesus eliminates all our conflicts and struggles is a cruel lie. Allowing the Bible to achieve its storied intent of transformation through relationship requires courage. It is as one allows the biblical narrative to be absorbed into one's "imagination as a story, not a manual," that gives one room to respect each other's formation in all of it unique particularities. With a healthy imagination, the bible becomes "a story to enter not a blueprint to follow."[8]

5. Lewis, *Of Other Worlds*, 37.
6. Miller, *Million Miles*, 180.
7. Bonheoffer, 105.
8. Peterson, *The Pastor*, 120.

10

Conclusion

As one begins to grapple with what it means to live a storied life, one realizes that the whole story begins and ends with great goodness, abounding. It is not humanities task to prepare for the return of Christ, doing our part in participating in the establishment of his kingdom. Our charge is to become a people fully alive, participating in his kingdom-making activity. Character transformation is not only the purpose of a story, it is the point of life. It was not Job's respectability, fabulous wealth, or great family that caught the attention of heaven and earth; it was the integrity of Job's character that caught the attention of heaven and earth (Job ch.1–2). Remembering always that "a good storyteller, . . . invites other people into the story . . . giving them a better story too,"[1] helping one to realize this most gracious narrative reveals that all God really wants from us is to live in our divinely made bodies, placing us in our neighborhoods at this time to be worshipers of him, participating in his creative activity that we are surrounded by. It is in finding our place in his story, finding joy in our relationships, experiencing his sheer pleasure in redeeming and transforming us, and usually this begins long before we are aware of it.

Living in Prince Albert means living in a town where violent crimes are on the rise. According to the Canadian Centre for

---

1. Miller, *Million Miles*, 236.

Conclusion

Justice Statistics, in 2010 we were ranked third among cities its size for violent crimes; in 2009, we were fourth. In 2011, in a city with just over 40,000 residents, there were almost 10,000 drunk and disorderly arrests, and violations causing deaths have risen 150 percent from 2010 to 2012. Likewise, from 2010 to 2011, reported sexual assaults were up 26 percent and prostitution arrests were up 93 percent,[2] both of which former Police Chief Dale McFee believes are a result of alcohol or drug problems. It is estimated that over 80 percent of the crimes in Prince Albert are drug or alcohol related.[3] In a new report, posted September 23, 2015, by *The 10 and 3*, the Prince Albert Parkland Health Region is ranked as the unhealthiest region in Canada, with only 63 percent of the region considered in "good perceived mental health" and over a quarter of the population on reserve living with diabetes. Characterizing this region as a one suffering from "endemic poverty, disadvantaged First Nations Communities, an aging population and a lack of doctor."[4]

These statistics tell a story that the Prince Albert area is in crisis and conflict. This is not an imagined reality, and how one responds or participates in the crisis can make the difference of life or death. As a pastor in Prince Albert, with the help of my increased understanding and appreciation for the power of the Biblical Narrative, I am encouraged. Great stories are shared in conflict while I live in a place of great opportunity to participate in the transformational narrative of Scripture. Specifically, how can I continue to live as a follower of Jesus here in this place, at this time?

For me, this begins with being encouraged by Job's tenacious refusal to curse God or to give up. "Naked I came from my mother's womb, naked I'll return to the womb of the earth. God gives, God takes. God's name be ever blessed. Not once through all this did Job sin; not once did he blame God" (Job 1:22–23). Job

2. http://papolice.ca/Portals/CrimeStat/PAPS/CrimeStat.2011.pdf.
3. http://www.panow.com/node/178868.
4. http://www.the10and3.com/do-you-live-in-one-of-the-unhealthiest-places-in-canada/.

shows one "how to push through protests in the face of suffering and get through the pain to a more intensely lived faith."[5] I cannot deny that this is a dangerous place to raise my family, but this is the place God has called me to. This gives me the freedom to agree with Miller when he calls out the escapist, protectionist lie that Jesus Christ will make everything better. He doesn't. "Jesus is not a get out of jail free" card; yes, ultimately Jesus does realize his kingdom, but it is not my responsibility to bring about the return of Christ or to establish his kingdom, it is his. My task is to become a fully alive person, living in the story of Christ's kingdom-making activity. God ordered the world so that the local, personal, relational human body is the primary place one gets to know God. I need to stop reading the Bible for answers and continue falling in love with the revelation of a God who is love, with us, present and active: It is in opening up myself to the transforming and transfiguring activity of God, reading Scripture, and engaging in this place with pregnant expectation, trusting the master storyteller, learning to find my place in the story.

Over the last few years with the community I worship with, we have been learning together what it means to find our place in the story of God's redemption activity in Prince Albert, Saskatchewan. We began asking ourselves, what is the ministry God has equipped and called us to join him in? We are a typical congregation, struggling to make the finances work, and struggling to see our way forward. So we ask ourselves not what it is that we want, but ask ourselves what it is that we have to offer to God for his use in the kingdom? We have a few women who enjoy knitting, a few amazing cooks, a few parents longing for their children to return to church, a few bringing their children or grandchildren to Sunday school, and a building mostly unused during the week.

We are still a congregation challenged with limited resources, both human and financal: we had to replace our roof recently, and we are struggling to see our way forward. But we have been invited into some amazing opportunities. The women who love knitting have begun knitting prayer shawls and giving them away to people

---

5. Peterson, *The Message Study Bible*, 718.

Conclusion

facing health, and this group is now teaching others how to knit, as well as making toques and knits for kids at a local elementary school. The group that loves cooking and serving food is participating in feeding over 150 hungry people one Saturday a month, and the number of people who are participating in this ministry is growing. A few who have a heart for prisoners are picking up inmates, so that they can attend public worship and other meetings. A few men heard of a need for wooden cross necklaces, and have hand-crafted over a thousand black walnut cross necklaces in responding to that need, to be given away at the local maximum security prison. 12-step recovery groups now use our building four to five nights a week. A Bible study group birthed a suicide prevention initiative that has been used throughout Saskatchewan, resulting in suicide prevention officers and social workers being hired, and suicide intervention training occurring.

What does reading scripture and engaging in your place with pregnant expectation, trusting the master storyteller, look like in your place? I don't know. What I do know is that God has uniquely placed you in your worshipping community. Do you see yourself participating in God's story of redemption and transformation? What part of God's redemption story have you been prepared for and are you participating in?
As Justin Welby, the Archbishop of Canterbury, said in an interview with Nicky Gumbel, "We are what we are before God and nothing more . . . it's all grace . . . We need to be a risk-taking church . . . there is no safety in Christ, there is absolute security . . . there is a big difference between knowing we are in his arms and knowing that he calls us to do risky things . . . we cannot live for our cause to win, we have to live for [Jesus'] cause to win."[6]

---

6. http://www.archbishopofcanterbury.org/articles.php/5059/watch-we-need-to-be-a-risk-taking-church-archbishop-opens-international-christian-conference.

Bibliography

Aaronovitch, David. *Voodoo Histories: The Role of the Conspiracy Theory in Shaping Modern History.* New York: Riverhead, 2010.
Ackerman, Dianne "The Brain on Love." In *New York Times*, March 24, 2012. http://opinionator.blogs.nytimes.com/2012/03/24/the-brain-on-love.
Adler, J. M. and D. P. McAdams. "Time, Culture, and Stories of the Self." In *Psychological Inquiry* 18, no. 2 (2007): 97–99.
Admirand, Peter. *Amidst Mass Atrocity and the Rubble of Theology: Searching for a Viable Theodicy.* Eugene: Cascade, 2012.
Alter, Robert. *The Art of Biblical Narrative.* New York: Basic, 1981.
———. *The Art of Biblical Poetry.* New York: Basic, 1985.
———. *Canon and Creativity: Modern Writing and the Authority of Scripture.* New Haven: Yale University Press, 2000.
———. *The David Story: A Translation with Commentary of 1 and 2 Samuel.* New York: W. W. Norton, 1999.
Alter, Robert, and Jane Alter. *The Transformative Power of Crisis: Our Journey to Psychological Healing and Spiritual Awakening.* London: Thorsons, 2000.
Alter, Robert and Frank Kermode eds. *The Literary Guide To The Bible.* Cambridge: Belknap Press of Harvard University Press, 1987.
Altizer, Thomas J. J. *The Descent into Hell: A Study of the Radical Reversal of the Christian Consciousness.* Philadelphia: Lippincott, 1970.
Anderson, Herbert. "How Rituals Heal." *Word & World* 30, no. 1 (2010): 41–50. ATLA Religion Database with ATLASerials, EBSCOhost.
Appiah, Kwame Anthony. *The Ethics of Identity.* Princeton: Princeton University Press, 2005.
Auster, Paul. *The Locked Room.* New York: Penguin, 1986.
Barkun, Michael. *A Culture of Conspiracy: Apocalyptic Visions in Contemporary America.* Series, *Comparative Studies in Religion and Society.* Berkley: University of California Press, 2013.
Bartholomew, Craig G., and Michael W. Goheen. *The Drama of Scripture: Finding Our Place in the Biblical Story.* Grand Rapids. Baker Academic, 2004.

BIBLIOGRAPHY

———. *The True Story of the Whole World: Finding Your Place in the Biblical Drama*. Grand Rapids: Faith Alive Christian Resources, 2009.

Bass, Diana Butler. *A People's History of Christianity: The Other Side of the Story*. New York: HarperOne, 2009.

———. *The Practicing Congregation: Imagining a New Old Church*. Herndon: Alban Institute, 2004.

Bauer, Jack J., et al. "Narrative Identity and Eudaimonic Well-Being." *Journal of Happiness Studies* 9, no. 1 (2008): 81–104.

Bellah, Robert Neelly. *Religion in Human Evolution: From the Paleolithic to the Axial Age*. Cambridge: Belknap Press of Harvard University Press, 2011.

Berger, Klaus. "Exegesis and the Unconscious Mind." In *Identity and Experience in the New Testament*, 18–23. Minneapolis: Fortress, 2003.

———. "Identity and Person." In *Identity and Experience in the New Testament*, 26–43. Minneapolis: Fortress, 2003.

Berry, Wendell. *Imagination in Place: Essays*. Berkeley: Counterpoint, 2010.

———. *Jayber Crow: A Novel*. Washington: Counterpoint, 2000.

———. *The Way of Ignorance: and Other Essays*. Emeryville: Shoemaker & Hoard, 2005.

Bettelheim, Bruno. *The Uses of Enchantment: the Meaning and Importance of Fairy Tales*. New York: Knopf, 1976.

Bock, Darrell L. *Recovering the Real Lost Gospel: Reclaiming the Gospel as Good News*. Waterville: Christian Large Print/Gale Cengage Learning, 2010.

Bonhoeffer, Dietrich. *Act and Being*. New York: Harper, 1962.

The Books of the Bible: A Presentation of Today's New International Version. Colorado Springs: Biblica, 2007.

Boyd, Brian. *On the Origin of Stories: Evolution, Cognition, and Fiction*. Cambridge: Belknap Press of Harvard University Press, 2009.

Bright, John. *The Kingdom of God: The Biblical Concept and Its Meaning for the Church*. Nashville: Abingdon-Cokesbury, 1953.

Brooks, David. *The Social Animal: The Hidden Sources of Love, Character, and Achievement*. New York: Random House, 2011.

Brooks, Peter. *Reading for the Plot: Design and Intention in Narrative*. Cambridge: Harvard University Press, 1992.

Brown, David. *Tradition and Imagination: Revelation and Change*. Oxford: Oxford University Press, 2004.

Brown, Tim, and Barry Katz. *Change by Design: How Design Thinking Transforms Organizations and Inspires Innovation*. New York: Harper Business, 2009.

Bruce, Elizabeth McIsaac. "Narrative Inquiry: A Spiritual and Liberating Approach to Research." In *Religious Education* 103, no. 3 (2008): 323–38.

Brueggemann, Walter. *The Bible Makes Sense*. Cincinnati, OH: St. Anthony Messenger, 2003.

———. *An Unsettling God: The Heart of the Hebrew Bible*. Minneapolis: Fortress, 2009.

Bruner, Jerome S. *Actual Minds, Possible Worlds*. Cambridge: Harvard University Press, 1986.

BIBLIOGRAPHY

———. *On Knowing: Essays for the Left Hand.* Cambridge: Harvard University Press, 1979.

———. *Making Stories: Law, Literature, Life.* Cambridge: Harvard University Press, 2003.

Bryant, David J. *Faith and the Play of Imagination.* Macon: Mercer University Press, 1989.

Buber, Martin. *I and Thou.* New York: Scribner, 1958.

Burke, Peter J., and Jan E. Stets. *Identity Theory.* Oxford: Oxford University Press, 2009.

Buster, Bobette. "The Arc of Storytelling." Lecture, Q: Portland 2010, The Crystal Ballroom, Portland, April 28, 2011.

———. *Do Story: How to Tell Your Story so the World Listens.* The Do Book Company, 2013

———. Lecture Series, *Epiphany: the Art of the Transformational Narrative,* Crosby Street Screening Room, Crosby Street Hotel, New York City, October 11–12, 2011.

———. Lecture Series, *Epiphany: How Understanding Story Creates Change,* Tribeca Cinemas, New York City, October 4–5, 2012.

Coen, Enrico. *Cells to Civilizations: Principles of Change That Shape Life.* Princeton: Princeton University Press, 2012.

Cooke, Phil. *One Big Thing: Discovering What You Were Born to Do.* Nashville: Thomas Nelson, 2012.

Cooley, C. H. *Human Nature and the Social Order.* New York: Scribner, 1902.

Coley, Brian. "Evolution of a Voice." Lecture, Q: Portland, 2010, The Crystal Ballroom, Portland, April 28, 2011.

Conradie, Ernst M. "How Are They Telling the Story? Reflections on Variations on a Theme: An Editorial." *Scriptura: International Journal of Bible, Religion and Theology in South Africa* 97 (2008): 1–12.

Cornejo, Marcela. "Political Exile and the Construction of Identity: A Life Stories Approach." In *Journal of Community & Applied Social Psychology* 18, no. 4 (2008): 333–48.

Crouch, Andy. "Power." Lecture, Andrew Mellon Auditorium, Washington, April 10, 2012.

Damasio, Antonio. *Self Comes to Mind: Constructing the Conscious Brain.* New York: Pantheon, 2010.

Denning, Stephen. *The Leader's Guide to Storytelling: Mastering the Art and Discipline of Business Narrative.* San Francisco: Jossey-Bass/A Wiley, 2005.

———. *The Secret Language of Leadership: How Leaders Inspire Action through Narrative.* San Francisco: Jossey-Bass, 2007.

———. *The Springboard: How Storytelling Ignites Action in Knowledge-era Organizations.* Boston: Butterworth-Heinemann, 2001.

———. *Squirrel Inc.: A Fable of Leadership through Storytelling.* San Francisco: Jossey-Bass, 2004.

Dillard, Annie. *Pilgrim at Tinker Creek.* East Sussex: Gardner, 2011.

Bibliography

Doehring, Carrie. *The Practice of Pastoral Care: A Postmodern Approach.* Louisville: Westminster John Knox, 2006.

Doerrer-Peacock, Barbara. *Space, Symbol, and Story: Windows to Transformation.* Dissertation, Pacific School of Religion, 2008.

Downing, Crystal. *Changing Signs of Truth: A Christian Introduction to the Semiotics of Communication.* Downers Grove: Intervarsity Academic, 2012.

Duhigg, Charles. *The Power of Habit: Why We Do What We Do and How to Change It.* New York: Random, 2012.

Erikson, Erik H. *Childhood and Society.* New York: Norton, 1978.

Filipp, Jacob, et al. "Do You Live in One of the Unhealthiest Places in Canada?" http://www.the10and3.com/do-you-live-in-one-of-the-unhealthiest-places-in-canada.

Fivush, Robyn, et al. "'Do You Know . . .': The Power of Family History in Adolescent Identity and Well-Being. http://www.journaloffamilylife.org/print/node/518.html.

Foster, Richard J., and Kathryn A. Helmers. *Life with God: Reading the Bible for Spiritual Transformation.* New York: HarperLuxe, 2008.

Frankl, Victor Emil. *Trotzdem Ja Zum Leben Sagen: Ein Psychologe erlebt das Konzentrationlager*, 1946.

———. *Man's Search for Meaning: An Introduction to Logotherapy.* New York: Pocket, 1963.

Frei, Hans. "Identity Description and Jesus Christ." In *Theology after Liberalism: A Reader*, edited by J. B. Webster and George P. Schner, 65–86. Oxford: Blackwell, 2000.

Frye, Northrup. *The Educated Imagination.* Toronto: Anansi, 1993.

Gadamer, H. *Truth and Method.* London: Continuum, 2004.

Ganzevoort, R. Ruard. "Scars and Stigmata: Trauma, Identity and Theology." In *Practical Theology* 1, no. 1, (2008).

Gazzaniga, Michael S. *Who's in Charge?: Free Will and the Science of the Brain.* New York: HarperCollins, 2011.

Gergen, Kenneth J. *The Saturated Self: Dilemmas of Identity in Contemporary Life.* New York: Basic, 1991.

Gladding, Sean. *The Story of God, the Story of Us: Getting Lost and Found in the Bible.* Downers Grove: IVP, 2010

Godin, Seth. *Tribes: We Need You to Lead Us.* New York: Portfolio, 2008.

Goffee, Robert, and Gareth Jones. *Why Should Anyone Be Led by You?: What It Takes to Be an Authentic Leader.* Boston: Harvard Business School Press, 2006.

Goheen, Michael W. *A Light to the Nations: The Missional Church and the Biblical Story.* Grand Rapids: Baker Academic, 2011.

———. "The Urgency of Reading the Bible as One Story." *Theology Today* 64, no. 4 (2008): 469–83.

Bibliography

Golemon, Larry A. "Reclaiming the Story: Narrative Leadership in Ministry." In *Congregations* 34, no. 1 (2008): 8. Quoting from Paul Auster. *The Locked Room*. New York: Penguin, 1986.

Gordon, Charlotte. *The Woman Who Named God: Abraham's Dilemma and the Birth of Three Faiths*. New York: Little Brown, 2009.

Gottschall, Jonathan. *The Storytelling Animal: How Stories Make Us Human*. Boston: Houghton Mifflin, Harcourt, 2012.

Graham, Stedman. *Identity: Your Passport to Success*. Upper Saddle River, NJ: Financial Times/Prentice Hall, 2012.

Green, Garrett. *Imagining God: Theology and Religious Imagination*. San Fransisco: Harper and Row, 1989.

Greer, Rowan A. *Anglican Approaches to Scripture: From the Reformation to the Present*. New York: Crossroad, 2006.

Guber, Peter. *Tell to Win: Connect, Persuade, and Triumph with the Hidden Power of Story*. New York: Crown Business, 2011.

Habermas, Tilmann. *The Development of Autobiographical Reasoning in Adolescence and Beyond*. San Francisco: Jossey-Bass, 2011.

Hanhardt, Richard W. *Sacred Bond: A Model of Spiritual Transformation for Therapists, Clients, and Seekers*. Bloomington: Westbow, 2012.

Hart, David Bentley. *The Experience of God: Being Consciousness, Bliss*. New Haven: Yale University Press, 2013.

Hartley, James Robert. *The Story as an Educational Form for the Church*. Thesis, School of Theology at Claremont, 1978.

Harvey, Anthony E. "Christian Propositions and Christian Stories." In *God Incarnate: Story and Belief*, edited by Anthony E. Harvey, 1–13. London: SPCK, 1981.

Hauerwas, Stanley, and L. Gregory. Jones, eds. *Why Narrative?: Readings in Narrative Theology*. Grand Rapids: W.B. Eerdmans, 1989.

Hoffman, Lawrence A. "Principle, Story, and Myth in the Liturgical Search for Identity." In *Interpretation* 64, no. 3 (2010): 231–44.

Hogan, Patrick Colm. *The Mind and Its Stories: Narrative Universals and Human Emotion*. Cambridge: Cambridge University Press, 2003.

Hood, Bruce M. *The Self Illusion: How the Social Brain Creates Identity*. Oxford: Oxford University Press, 2012.

———. *Supersense: Why We Believe in the Unbelievable*. New York: HarperOne, 2009.

Hoyt, Timothy. "The Development of Narrative Identity in Late Adolescence and Emergent Adulthood: The Continued Importance of Listeners." In *Developmental Psychology*, Vol. 45, No. 2 (2009).

Huettel, S. A., et al. *Functional Magnetic Resonance Imaging*. 2nd ed. Massachusetts: Sinauer, 2009.

Jacobs, Alan. *A Theology of Reading: The Hermeneutics of Love*. Boulder: Westview, 2001.

James, William. *Talks to Teachers of Psychology and to Students on Some of Life's Ideals*. Cambridge: Harvard University Press, 1983.

Bibliography

Jenkins, Richard. *Social Identity*. Abingdon: Routledge, 2008.

Jensen, Robert W. *Face to Face: Portraits of the Divine in Early Christianity*. Minneapolis: Fortress, 2005.

———. "How the World Lost Its Story: As Our Changing Culture Struggled to Define itself, the Theologian Robert W. Jenson Mourned the Missing Narrative of a Universe Gone Postmodern And Mad." *First Things* no. 201 (2010): 31–37.

Josipovici, Gabriel. *The Singer on the Shore: Essays 1991–2004*. Manchester: Carcanet, 2006.

Jungel, Eherhard. *God as the Mystery of the World*. Grand Rapids: Eerdmans. Trans. Darrell Gruder, 1983.

Kaiser, Walter C. *Recovering the Unity of the Bible: One Continuous Story, Plan, and Purpose*. Grand Rapids: Zondervan, 2009.

Keller, Timothy. *King's Cross: The Story of the World in the Life of Jesus*. New York: Dutton, 2011.

Kelly, John Francis, and Mark G. Meyers. "Adolescents' Participation in Alcoholics Anonymous and Narcotics Anonymous: Review, Implications, and Future Directions." In *Journal of Psychoactive Drugs* 39, no 3 (2007): 259–69.

Kelly, John Francis, et al. "How do Peoples Recover from Alcoholic Dependence: A Systematic Review of the Research on the Mechanisms of Behavior Change in Alcoholics Anonymous." In *Addiction Research and Theory* 17, no. 3 (2009): 236–59.

Kermode, Frank. *The Genesis of Secrecy: On the Interpretation of Narrative*. Cambridge: Harvard University Press, 1979.

King, Laura. "The Hard Road to the Good Life: The Happy, Mature Person." In *Journal of Humanistic Psychology* 41, (2001): 58.

Kreeft, Peter. *An Ocean Full of Angels: The Autobiography of 'Isa Ben Adam*. South Bend: St. Augustine's, 2011.

Landau, Elizabeth. "What the Brain Draws from: Art and Neuroscience." *CNN. com*, November 6, 2012. http://www.cnn.com/2012/11/06/health/art-brain-mind-nov/index.html?hpt=hp_rr_7.

Lawler, Steph. *Identity: Sociological Perspectives*. Cambridge: Polity, 2008.

Le Grys, Alan. "Shaped by God's Story: Making Sense of the Bible." Thesis, King's College London, 2008.

Lewis, C. S. *Of Other Worlds: Essays and Stories*. New York: Harcourt Brace Jovanovich, 1975.

Lints, Richard, et al. *Personal Identity in Theological Perspective*. Grand Rapids: William B. Eerdmans Pub, 2006.

Loughlin, Gerard. *Telling God's Story: Bible, Church, and Narrative Theology*. Cambridge: Cambridge University Press, 1996.

Lyons, Gabe, and Norton Herbst. *The Next Christians: Following Jesus in a Post-Christian Culture*. Grand Rapids: Zondervan, 2011.

Lyotard, Jean-Francois. *The Postmodern Condition: A Report on Knowledge*. Minneapolis: University of Minneapolis Press, 1979.

BIBLIOGRAPHY

Maalouf, Amin. *On Identity*. London: Harvill, 2000.
Maier, S. F. and L. R. Watkins. "Stressor Controllability, Anxiety and Serotonin." In *Cognitive Therapy Research*, 22 (1998): 595–613.
MacDonald, Mark L. Interview by author. October 4, 2011.
Marek, Kate. *Organizational Storytelling for Librarians: Using Stories for Effective Leadership*. Chicago: American Library Association, 2011.
Martin, Timothy. "Illuminating the Landscape of Religious Narrative: Morality, Dramatization, and Verticality." In *Religious Education* 104, no. 4 (2009): 393–405.
Martoia, Ron. *Transformational Architecture: Reshaping Our Lives as Narrative*. Grand Rapids: Zondervan, 2008.
McAdams, Dan P., and Jennifer L. Pals. "A New Big Five: Fundamental Principles for an Integrative Science of Personality." In *American Psychologist* 61, no. 3 (2006): 204–17.
McAdams, Dan P. *Power, Intimacy, and the Life Story: Personological Inquiries into Identity*. Homewood: Dorsey, 1985.
———. "The Psychology of Life Stories." In *Review of General Psychology* 5, no. 2 (2001): 100–122.
———. *The Redemptive Self: Stories Americans Live By*. Oxford: Oxford University Press, 2006.
McAdams, Dan P., et al. *Identity and Story: Creating Self in Narrative*. Washington: American Psychological Association, 2006.
McCracken, David. *The Scandal of the Gospels: Jesus, Story, and Offense*. New York: Oxford University Press, 1994.
McKnight, Scot. *The Blue Parakeet: Rethinking How You Read the Bible*. Grand Rapids: Zondervan, 2008.
———. *The King Jesus Gospel: The Original Good News Revisited*. Grand Rapids: Zondervan, 2011.
McLaren, Brian D. *The Story We Find Ourselves In: Further Adventures of a New Kind of Christian*. San Francisco: Jossey-Bass, 2003.
McLean, Kate C. "Stories of the Young and the Old: Personal Continuity and Narrative Identity." In *Developmental Psychology* 44, no. 1 (2008): 254–64.
McNeal, Reggie. *Get a Life!: It Is All about You*. Nashville: B & H Group, 2007.
Meltzoff, A. N., et al. "Foundations for a New Science of Learning." *Science* 325 (2009): 284–288.
Miller, Donald. "How Narrative Shapes Culture." Lecture, Q. Atlanta 2007, Atlanta, GA, April 2007. http://www.qideas.org/video/narrative-expressions.aspx.
———. *A Million Miles in a Thousand Years: What I Learned While Editing My Life*. Nashville: Thomas Nelson, 2010.
———. *Storyline 2.0: Finding Your Subplot in God's Story*. Portland: Donald Miller Words, 2012.
———. Storyline 2.0 Conference, Point Loma Nazarene University, San Diego, CA. February 23–24, 2013.

Bibliography

———. *Your Story Series*. Rec. 2010. Mellowtown, 2010. MP3.
Minear, Paul S. *Images of the Church in the New Testament*. London: James Clarke, 2007.
Mlodinow, Leonard. *Subliminal: How Your Unconscious Mind Rules Your Behavior*. New York: Pantheon, 2012.
Monterosso, John and Barry Schwatz. "Did Your Brain Make You Do It?" In *New York Times*, July 27, 2012.http://www.nytimes.com/2012/07/29/opinion/sunday/neuroscience-and-moral-responsibility.html.
Murphy, Francesca Aran. *God Is Not a Story: Realism Revisited*. Oxford: Oxford University Press, 2007.
Murphy Paul, Annie. "Your Brain on Fiction." In *New York Times*, March 17, 2012.http://www.nytimes.com/2012/03/18/opinion/sunday/the-neuroscience-of-your-brain-on-fiction.html?pagewanted=all.
Navone, John J., and John J. Navone. *Seeking God in Story*. Collegeville: Liturgical, 1990.
Nichols, Stephen J. and Eric T. Brandt. *Ancient Word, Changing Worlds: The Doctrine of Scripture in a Modern Age*. Wheaton: Crossway, 2009.
Onstot, Kenneth. *The Bible's Plot: Connecting the Bible's Story to Your Story*. St. Louis: Lucas Park, 2009.
Palmer, Parker J. *To Know as We Are Known: Education as a Spiritual Journey*. New York: HarperOne, 1993.
Pennebaker, James W. *The Secret Life of Pronouns: What Our Words Say about Us*. New York: Bloomsbury, 2011.
Perry, John. *Personal Identity*. Berkeley: University of California Press, 2008.
Peterson, Eugene H. *The Jesus Way: A Conversation on the Ways that Jesus is the Way*. Grand Rapids: Eerdmans, 2007.
———. *A Long Obedience in the Same Direction: Discipleship in an Instant Society*. Downers Grove: InterVarsity, 1980.
———. *The Message Study Bible: Capturing the Notes and Reflections of Eugene Peterson*. Colorado Springs, CO: Navpress Pub Group, 2012.
———. *The Pastor: A Memoir*. New York: Harper, 2011.
———. *Practice Resurrection: A Conversation on Growing up in Christ*. Grand Rapids: Eerdmans, 2011.
———. Lecture Series, *Practices: Cultivating your Inner Life in an Age of Distraction*, Crosby Street Screening Room, Crosby Street Hotel, February 28–29, 2012.
Placher, William. "The Triune God: The Perichoresis of Particular Persons." In *Theology after Liberalism: A Reader*, J. B. Webster and George P. Schner, eds. Oxford: Blackwell, 2000, 87–106.
Quart, Alissa. "Neuroscience under Attack." In *New York Times*, November 23, 2012.http://www.nytimes.com/2012/11/25/opinion/sunday/neuroscience-under-attack.html.
Räisänen, Heikki. *Beyond New Testament Theology: A Story and a Programme*. London: SCM, 2000.

Bibliography

Ranaghan, Dorothy. *Blind Spot: War and Christian Identity*. Hyde Park: New City, 2011.

Rand, Ayn. *For the New Intellectual: The Philosophy of Ayn Rand*. New York: Random House, 1961.

Randall, W. L. "From Compost to Computer: Rethinking our Metaphors for Memory." In *Theory Psychology* 17 (2007): 611–33.

Robinson, Marilynne. *Absence of Mind: The Dispelling of Inwardness from the Modern Myth of the Self*. New Haven: Yale University Press, 2010.

Roediger III, H. L. and K. B. McDermott. "Tricks of Memory." In *Current Directions in Psychological Science* 9 (2000): 123–27.

Rossow, Justin. "Preaching the Story Behind the Image: The Homiletical Fruit of a Narrative Approach to Metaphor." *Concordia Journal* 34, no. 1 (2008): 9–21.

Sams, Drew. *The Re-Membered Church: Establishing and Enacting a Narrative Ecclesiology in a New Media World*. DMin dissertation, George Fox Evangelical Seminary, April 2012.

Schultz, Kathryn. *Being Wrong: Adventures in the Margin of Error*. New York: HarperCollins, 2010.

Schwartz, Barry. *The Paradox of Choice: Why More Is Less*. New York: HarperCollins, 2004.

Scott, Ian W., and Ian W. Scott. *Paul's Way of Knowing: Story, Experience, and the Spirit*. Grand Rapids: Baker Academic, 2009.

Searle, John R. *Freedom and Neurobiology: Reflections on Free Will, Language, and Political Power*. New York: Columbia University Press, 2007.

Segal, Jerome M. *Joseph's Bones: Understanding the Struggle between God and Mankind in the Bible*. New York: Riverhead, 2007.

Shermer, Michael. *The Believing Brain: From Spiritual Faiths to Political Convictions—How We Construct Beliefs and Reinforce Them as Truths*. London: Robinson, 2012.

Silverman, Lori L. *Wake Me Up When the Data Is Over: How Organizations Use Stories to Drive Results*. San Francisco: Jossey-Bass, 2006.

Simmons, Annette. *The Story Factor: Secrets of Influence from the Art of Storytelling*. New York: Basic, 2006.

———. *Whoever Tells the Best Story Wins: How to Use Your Own Stories to Communicate with Power and Impact*. New York: Amacom, 2007.

Smith, Christian. *The Bible Made Impossible: Why Biblicism Is Not a Truly Evangelical Reading of Scripture*. Grand Rapids: Brazos, 2011.

Smith, James K. A. *Desiring the Kingdom: Worship, Worldview, and Cultural Formation*. Grand Rapids: Baker Academic, 2009.

———. *Imagining the Kingdom: How Worship Works*, Grand Rapids: Baker Academic, 2013.

———. "Imagining the Kingdom." Lecture, Q, Andrew Mellon Auditorium, Washington, April 11, 2012.

———. *You are What You Love: The Spiritual Power of Habit*. Grand Rapids: Brazos, 2016.

Bibliography

Snodgrass, Klyne. "Reading to Hear: A Hermeneutic of Hearing." *Horizons in Biblical Theology* 24 (2002).

Song, Choan-Seng. *In the Beginning Were Stories, Not Texts: Story Theology.* Eugene: Cascade, 2011.

Sotgiu I., and C. Mormont. "Similarities and Differences Between Traumatic and Emotional Memories: Review and Directions for Future Research." In *Journal Of Psychology [serial online]* 142, no. 5 (2008):449–70.

Spadaro, Antonio. "A Big Heart Open to God." http://americamagazine.org/pope-interview.

Spawn, Kevin L., and Archie T. Wright. *Spirit and Scripture: Exploring a Pneumatic Hermeneutic.* London: T & T Clark, 2012.

Spong, John Shelby. *Re-Claiming the Bible for a Non-Religious World.* New York: HarperOne, 2011.

Strawson, Galen. "The Unstoried Life." In *On Life Writing*, Zachary Leader eds. Oxford University Press, 2015.

Strauss, Gideon. "Principled Pluralism." Lecture, Q, Andrew Mellon Auditorium, Washington, April 10, 2012.

Stroup, George W. "Theology of Narrative or Narrative Theology: A Response to Why Narrative?" In *Theology Today* 47, no. 4 (1991): 424–32.

Stutz, Phil and Barry Michels. *The Tools: Transform your Problems into Courage, Confidence, and Creativity.* New York: Random House, 2012.

Swartley, Willard M. *Israel's Scripture Traditions and the Synoptic Gospels: Story Shaping Story.* Grand Rapids: Baker Academic, 1993.

Sweet, Leonard I. *I Am a Follower: The Way, Truth, and Life of following Jesus.* Nashville: Thomas Nelson, 2012.

———. "Introduction to Semiotics." Lecture, *Semiotics and Future Studies Orientation Advance*, Paramount Hotel, Portland, August 25, 2011.

———. *Nudge: Awakening Each Other to the God Who's Already There.* Colorado Springs, CO: David C. Cook, 2010.

———. *Strong in the Broken Places: A Theological Reverie on the Ministry of George Everett Ross.* Akron: University of Akron Press, 1995.

———. *So Beautiful: Divine Design for Life and the Church: Missional, Relational, Incarnational.* Colorado Springs, CO: David C. Cook, 2009.

———. *What Matters Most: How We Got the Point but Missed the Person.* Colorado Springs, CO: WaterBrook, 2012.

Sweet, Leonard I., and Edward H. Hammett. *The Gospel According to Starbucks: Living with a Grande Passion.* Colorado Springs: Waterbrook, 2007.

Sweet, Leonard I. and Frank Viola. *Jesus Manifesto: Restoring the Supremacy and Sovereignty of Jesus Christ.* Nashville: Thomas Nelson, 2010.

———. *Jesus: A Theography.* Nashville: Thomas Nelson, 2012.

Taylor, Mark C. "Disappearance of the Self." *Erring: A Postmodern A/theology.* Chicago: University of Chicago Press, 1984.

Tolkien, J. R. R. *Tree and Leaf and the Homecoming of Beorhtnoth.* New York: Harper Collins, 2001.

Bibliography

Turkle, Sherry. *Alone Together: Why We Expect More from Technology and Less from Each Other*. New York: Basic, 2011.

Underwood, Ralph. "Wincott's Squiggles Game and Biblical Interpretation." In *Psychological Insight into the Bible*, W. G. Rollins and D. A. Killie, eds. Grand Rapids: Eerdmans, 2007.

Van Huyssteen, J. Wentzel. *Alone in the World?: Human Uniqueness in Science and Theology*. Grand Rapids: Eerdmans, 2006.

Volf, Miroslav. *Exclusion and Embrace: A Theological Exploration of Identity, Otherness, and Reconciliation*. Nashville: Abingdon, 1996.

Wainwright, Geoffrey. *Doxology: the Praise of God in Worship, Doctrine, and Life: a Systematic Theology*. New York: Oxford University Press, 1980.

Wegener, Mark I. *Cruciformed: The Literary Impact of Mark's Story of Jesus and His Disciples*. Lanham: University Press of America, 1995.

White, Michael. *Maps of Narrative Practice*, New York: Norton, 2007.

Willard, Dallas. *Renovation of the Heart: Putting on the Character of Christ*. Colorado Springs, CO: NavPress, 2002.

Willard, Timothy D., and R. Jason Locy. *Veneer: Living Deeply in a Surface Society*. Grand Rapids: Zondervan, 2011.

Williams, Rowan. *The Edge of Words: God and the Habits of Language*. New York: Bloomsbury, 2014.

———. *Silence and Honey Cakes: The Wisdom of the Desert*. Oxford: Lion, 2007.

———. *Where God Happens: Discovering Christ in One Another*. Boston: New Seeds, 2005.

———. *Why Study the Past?: The Quest for the Historical Church*. Grand Rapids: Eerdmans, 2005.

———. *The Wound of Knowledge: Christian Spirituality from the New Testament to St. John of the Cross*. Cambridge: Cowley, 1990.

Witherington, Ben. *The Indelible Image: The Theological and Ethical Thought World of the New Testament*. Downers Grove: IVP Academic, 2010. 33–202.

Wright, Christopher J. H. *The Mission of God: Unlocking the Bible's Grand Narrative*. Downers Grove: IVP Academic, 2006.

Wright, N.T. *After You Believe: Why Christian Character Matters*. San Francisco: Harper, 2010.

———. "How Can The Bible Be Authoritative" http://ntwrightpage.com/Wright_Bible_Authoritative.htm.

———. *How God Became King: The Forgotten Story of the Gospels*. New York: HarperOne, 2012.

———. *Scripture and the Authority of God: How to Read the Bible Today*. New York: HarperOne, 2011.

Yandell, Keith E. *Faith and Narrative*. Oxford: Oxford University Press, 2001.

Yong, Amos. *Spirit of Love: A Trinitarian Theology of Grace*. Waco: Baylor University Press, 2012.

BIBLIOGRAPHY

Zornberg, Avivah Gottlieb. *The Murmuring Deep: Reflections on the Biblical Unconscious.* New York: Schocken, 2009.

Lightning Source UK Ltd.
Milton Keynes UK
UKOW06f0706260516

274981UK00001B/62/P

9 781498 219884